YORK NOTES

Oranges Are Not the Only Fruit

Jeanette Winterson

Note by Kathryn Simpson

 Longman   York Press

YORK PRESS
322 Old Brompton Road, London SW5 9JH

PEARSON EDUCATION LIMITED
Edinburgh Gate, Harlow,
Essex CM20 2JE, United Kingdom
Associated companies, branches and representatives throughout the world

First published 2001

ISBN 0–582–43157–3

Designed by Vicki Pacey
Phototypeset by Gem Graphics, Trenance, Mawgan Porth, Cornwall
Colour reproduction and film output by Spectrum Colour
Produced by Addison Wesley Longman China Limited, Hong Kong

CONTENTS

PART ONE

INTRODUCTION | How to Study a Novel | 5
Reading *Oranges Are Not the Only Fruit* | 6

PART TWO

SUMMARIES & COMMENTARIES

Note on the Text | 8
Synopsis | 8
Detailed Summaries | 10
Genesis | 10
Exodus | 17
Leviticus | 24
Numbers | 28
Deuteronomy | 31
Joshua | 34
Judges | 40
Ruth | 43

PART THREE

CRITICAL APPROACHES

Characterisation | 50
Jeanette | 50
Jeanette's mother | 52
Elsie Norris | 54
Miss Jewsbury | 55
Melanie | 55
Katy | 56
The pastors | 56
Jeanette's father | 57
Mrs White and May | 57
Mrs Arkwright, the woman and Joe | 58
Themes | 59
Quest for identity | 59
Exile and return | 60
Sexuality | 61

Narrative Technique	63
Juxtaposition of narrative elements	64
Form and Structure	64
Genre	64
Realism and fantasy	65
Autobiographical fiction	67
Bildungsroman	67
Parody	68
Allusion	68
Humour	70
Language and Style	70

PART FOUR

TEXTUAL ANALYSIS

Text 1	73
Text 2	76
Text 3	80

PART FIVE

BACKGROUND

The Author and Her Works	85
Historical Context	91

PART SIX

CRITICAL HISTORY & BROADER PERSPECTIVES

Reception and Early Reviews	94
Feminist Approaches	95
Feminist Post-structuralist Approaches	96
Feminist Psychoanalytic Approaches	97
Chronology	99
Bibliography	103
Literary Terms	105
Author of this Note	110

PART ONE

INTRODUCTION

HOW TO STUDY A NOVEL

Studying a novel on your own requires self-discipline and a carefully thought-out work plan in order to be effective.

- You will need to read the novel more than once. Start by reading it quickly for pleasure, then read it slowly and thoroughly.
- On your second reading make detailed notes on the plot, characters and themes of the novel. Further readings will generate new ideas and help you to memorise the details of the story.
- Some of the characters will develop as the plot unfolds. How do your responses towards them change during the course of the novel?
- Think about how the novel is narrated. From whose point of view are events described?
- A novel may or may not present events chronologically: the time-scheme may be a key to its structure and organisation.
- What part do the settings play in the novel?
- Are words, images or incidents repeated so as to give the work a pattern? Do such patterns help you to understand the novel's themes?
- Identify what styles of language are used in the novel.
- What is the effect of the novel's ending? Is the action completed and closed, or left incomplete and open?
- Does the novel present a moral and just world?
- Cite exact sources for all quotations, whether from the text itself or from critical commentaries. Wherever possible find your own examples from the novel to back up your opinions.
- Always express your ideas in your own words.

This York Note offers an introduction to *Oranges Are Not the Only Fruit* and cannot substitute for close reading of the text and the study of secondary sources.

Oranges Are Not the Only Fruit is Jeanette Winterson's most popular novel. Since its publication in 1985, it has been read with pleasure, laughter and anger. It is perceived as a novel about the universal 'rite of passage' experience of growing up and finding identity. Jeanette's rebellion against her mother and church family is seen as a typical confrontation between the younger and older generations. It is also read as a story that deals with a specific set of experiences determined by a clash between belief and sexuality, and as a lesbian 'coming-out' story. Winterson herself sees it as a powerful novel that challenges the way people think and experience the world, that questions certainties and that invites the reader to see things anew, from another perspective:

> '*Oranges* is a threatening novel. It exposes the sanctity of family life as something
> of a sham; it illustrates by example that what the church calls love is actually
> psychosis and it dares to suggest that what makes life difficult for homosexuals is
> not their perversity but other people's. Worse, it does these things with such
> humour and lightness that those disposed not to agree find that they do'
> (Introduction, Vintage, 1991, p. xiii).

Not all readers agree with this assessment, but certainly the novel raises some thought-provoking questions about the nature of reality and identity. It undermines what may seem self-evident differences between fact and fiction, history and story, and puts into doubt any certainty we may have about what truth is and what we should believe. An obvious way that Winterson challenges our need to know what is true is in her refusal to classify her novel. As she says in the introduction, 'Is *Oranges* an autobiographical novel? No not at all and yes of course' (Introduction, p. xiv). It is a novel that blurs the boundaries between the generic forms of realism and fantasy in a way that destabilises our expectations and forces us to make sense of Jeanette's story in more than one way. Without the fantasy sections, the meaning we can make from Jeanette's realist story is much reduced. Simultaneously, however, the fantasy sections resist an absolute interpretation, and the meaning we make from them can only ever be ambiguous. The range of allusions to other texts, to Greek mythology, biblical figures and events, artists, poets, music and historical figures also add significant levels of meaning and irony, leading the reader to many possible interpretations. However, the insistence on openness and multiplicity, and the resistance to narrative closure are powerful because they refuse to limit and contain the narrative; they suggest that the story can go on beyond the ending of the novel.

Oranges is a novel that deals with many important issues, notably issues of power as it impacts on identity and sexuality. The power of individuals, institutions and of cultural narratives to determine experience is scrutinised and exposed. Issues of tolerance, acceptance of difference, definitions of what is morally good, authority and the process and framing of interpretation are provocatively raised. The practice of revisionary storytelling offers a way to escape or at least to modify the limitations imposed on individuals as a consequence of their gender, sexuality, class and system of belief. It is with comic parody and cutting irony that Jeanette's mother, the church and the power hierarchies enshrined in the cultural narratives of biblical myth, fairy tale and official history are subverted, and their authority undermined. 'Trust me, I'm telling you stories' is the refrain in Winterson's novel *The Passion*. It points to the power that stories, which are not true but in which we can trust, have both to limit and liberate the imagination, a sense of identity and emotional and sexual expression.

Finally, *Oranges* is a trick of a novel. It raises profound issues with such lively wit that we might not realise that our perception and understanding of the world has subtly shifted. With humour that endears the reader to the central character, the novel undermines and revises stereotypical representations of women, and specifically of lesbian sexuality. It also puts notions of truth into question and makes the case for a relative and multiple sense of reality.

PART TWO

SUMMARIES & COMMENTARIES

Oranges Are Not the Only Fruit was first published in 1985 by Pandora Press; the edition used for this Note was published by Vintage in 1991.

SYNOPSIS

Oranges Are Not the Only Fruit tells the story of a girl growing up in a northern, working-class industrial town, brought up by adoptive parents within an evangelical Christian community. As proof of her new-found faith, her mother adopts Jeanette in order to train her for a missionary life devoted to God. As a child, Jeanette is immersed in the life of the church, its members and activities, and its fundamentalist interpretation of the Bible forms the basis of her experience. Although she is made to feel that she is special, this experience is doubly isolating – belonging to such a close-knit and extremist faith isolates her from the world beyond it, and being the only child in a community of adults also leads to her being socially and emotionally alienated from her peers. When she is about seven years old, she becomes deaf due to an illness and her mother and the majority of the congregation assume that she is in a blissful state of holy rapture. Jeanette is left alone to work out what is wrong with her and to seek help; it is only when Miss Jewsbury forces Jeanette's mother to realise the seriousness of the child's condition that Jeanette gets any medical attention and real care. During her stay in the hospital, she would again have been left almost entirely alone had it not been for the kindness of Elsie Norris, who visits every day, tells her stories and introduces her to literature and art. Jeanette finds the fluffy animal decoration in the children's ward peculiar, which is an indication that her upbringing has left her ill-prepared for life in the world outside the church. It foreshadows her experience of school, where her atypical childhood brings an even greater sense of isolation and of being at odds with the world around her. Although initially she tries to make friends and throughout her school life works hard for some recognition and sense of acceptance from the teachers, she is only ever perceived as odd because her perceptions, preoccupations, language and behaviour are so different from those of other children and from the teachers. She resigns herself to being an outsider and comforts herself with the certainty, inspired by her faith, that she is right. However, as a child she also shows some dissension from biblical authority, as she rewrites biblical stories in Fuzzy Felt and drowns the animals in the Ark at Elsie's house.

As Jeanette gets older, she becomes a successful evangelical preacher. Although she realises that she does not entirely agree with all the theological doctrine the church espouses, this is insufficient to cause her to dissent from church teaching. At fourteen, Jeanette meets Melanie in the market place and falls in love with her. Melanie joins Jeanette's church and, in all innocence of the possibility of the church's objection, they begin a lesbian relationship. As their relationship continues, Jeanette does feel the need for secrecy, but in a confidential moment she tells her mother some of what she feels for Melanie. Her sense of uncertainty at this point in her life triggers the memory of her biological mother's visit and the shock of discovering that she is adopted. Shortly afterwards, Jeanette and Melanie are accused of sinful and 'unnatural passions' before the church congregation and urged to repent, which Melanie does immediately. Jeanette fights the interpretation of their relationship as sinful and seems to repent only after being prayed over for a whole day, locked in the parlour for two days without food or light, and exorcised of her demons. After this traumatic experience, followed by a brief and distressing night spent with Melanie, Jeanette develops glandular fever. While she is ill, her mother ransacks her room, destroying all evidence of Jeanette and Melanie's relationship.

Melanie leaves to go to university, Jeanette returns to her role as a preacher and life seems to return to its normal round of church activities. During a week-long mission in Blackpool, Jeanette meets and becomes close to Katy, who has newly converted to the church. At Christmas Melanie returns and attempts to renew her friendship with Jeanette. This brings Jeanette's repressed feelings to the surface and shortly afterwards she and Katy begin a lesbian relationship. When this relationship is discovered, Jeanette is once again urged to renounce her sin, but this time refuses to give in to pressure from her mother and the congregation, and decides to leave the church. Angry and unable to accept Jeanette's sexuality, her mother forces her to leave home. She works selling ice-creams and in a funeral parlour. Elsie dies, and shortly afterwards Jeanette gets a job in a psychiatric hospital and eventually moves to another city. One Christmas she visits her parents. Her mother tells her of the scandals and corruption that have rocked the church, and shows off her CB radio – her new-found means of continuing her own vigorous role as 'missionary on the home front'. The novel ends on a note of irony as Jeanette's mother, easily enraged as ever, storms into the house to commence her CB radio broadcast as Kindly Light.

GENESIS   **Jeanette's adoption, an impression of her childhood, and key incidents of her seventh year; ends with Jeanette being on the point of going to school for the first time**

In this opening chapter we find out about Jeanette's adoption into a fundamentalist Christian family in a northern, working-class town. The narrative shifts between a recollection of typical and often repeated activities to focus on the events of one particular Sunday when Jeanette was seven. We are given details of the routine activities of Sundays, 'the most vigorous day of the whole week', which are dictated by her mother's devotion to her faith. These include her mother's morning prayers, the cup of tea made by Jeanette at exactly the right time, the notes on the missionary report broadcast on the radio, Sunday dinner, and Jeanette and her mother's afternoon walk with the dog.

Jeanette's memories of key incidents of the past are recalled as she and her mother walk up the hill. Jeanette's memory of a fairground gypsy's prophesy that she 'will never marry...and...never be still' is followed immediately by the memory of the day her mother forbade her to go to the local paper shop owned by two unmarried (implicitly lesbian) women (p. 7). These incidents and the way that they are linked in the narrative hint at the possibility of a lesbian sexuality for Jeanette.

The specific events of one particular Sunday are also described in this chapter. Her father breaks the rules and routines of Sundays by watching the wrestling on the television, and a visiting speaker, Pastor Roy Finch, gives a sermon on the deviousness of the Devil. Jeanette is taken as an example – 'This little lily could herself be a house of demons' – but escapes to the Sunday School Room and begins to play with the Fuzzy Felt (p. 12). The pastor interrupts and corrects Jeanette's subversive rewrite of Daniel in the Lion's Den, and begins to play with the Fuzzy Felt himself. On the way home from the church, Jeanette, her mother, Alice and May pay a brief visit to Mrs Arkwright's shop. The chapter ends with the receipt of a letter requiring Jeanette to attend school.

A strong impression of the time and environment in which Jeanette grows up is vividly conveyed by the description of the setting, the representative incidents and routine activities mentioned here. We are left in no doubt about the centrality of religion in this household. Most of the activities revolve around Jeanette's mother's rigid beliefs and her rigorous enforcement of them, and everything else is seen through the filter of fundamentalist Christianity. Her mother's religion is all-pervasive and her dogmatic views and confrontational attitude have a tremendous impact on Jeanette and her sense of the world, 'I had been brought in to join her in a tag match against the Rest of the World' (p. 3) and 'I discovered that everything in the natural world was a symbol of the Great Struggle between good and evil' (p. 16). Jeanette's education in terms of reading and gaining knowledge of the world stems from her mother's interests and obsessions – Jeanette learns to read from the Book of Deuteronomy in the Bible and gains an understanding of the wider world from seed catalogues. These source materials, coupled with a life restricted to church activities, do not bode well for Jeanette's integration into school and anticipate the problems ahead.

Jeanette's mother's dogmatic, narrow-minded views are consistently undercut in this chapter and throughout the novel by the use of mocking humour. The way that her mother's conversion story is related mocks her faith by belittling this all-important moment in her mother's life with the suggestion that the motivation for her faith is far from purely spiritual or moral. Instead of her conversion being marked by a moment of spiritual revelation, it is initially driven by material gain (a flowering cactus and the hope of a lily of the valley when her husband converts) and by her attraction to Pastor Spratt. Looking like Errol Flynn and depicted as an action-hero type of missionary, he is both 'holy' and Hollywood, and his charisma is an effective 'bait' for the many women 'who found the Lord that week' (p. 8). However, this conversion is also revealed to be a pragmatic decision, offering her a way of pursuing her fierce ambition, despite the fact that her life is one of increasingly reduced options.

The first fairy tale **allegorically** develops this exploration of the reasons for her mother's adoption of her faith and of Jeanette. However, it frames the 'brilliant' princess's decision differently – not as a necessity, but as a 'calling' and as a better alternative to a trivial life (see Part 3, p. 66). This is followed by a more realistic expression of her plans to realise her dream of the future. This version of the decision-making process combines both the pragmatic and the idealistic reasons she has already given for her actions, but adds another twist in that this decision is also now framed as a moral one. Like Pastor Spratt's calculated approach to conversions, Jeanette's mother is calculating about her adoption of Jeanette; it is not a result of maternal feeling, but of her need to find a role and to forge a future for herself. Jeanette is to be her mother's apprentice, and the older narrator cynically sums up what this means for her mother: 'She had a way out now for years and years to come' (p. 10). She no longer has to feel the shame of being disowned by her family, of being poor, with only limited options and a sense of inferiority.

Although there are moments in the novel when Jeanette's mother does show maternal love for Jeanette (in this chapter, for example, when Jeanette gets up in the night and they have bacon and eggs and read the Bible, p. 15), for the most part she seems cold and unaffectionate. This is in contrast to the way that other women treat and 'mother' Jeanette. In this first chapter, the gypsies and the women in the paper shop act as foils to Jeanette's mother. Their kindness to and nurturing of Jeanette with treats contrasts with her mother's largely severe and unloving attitude. Importantly, they also offer options for Jeanette's future, which, with their suggestion of lesbian sexuality, radically contradict her mother's plans and beliefs. Jeanette's alliance with these people counteracts

her mother's dogmatic views and intolerance, and anticipates
Jeanette's subsequent conflict with her mother and the church.
Later Elsie will also prove an important mother figure for Jeanette.

The period in which this novel is set is also established here
by reference to household items and radio programmes, and
through a sense of what is happening in the wider world. The
setting of the novel in a northern, working-class town is also
firmly established. The panoramic view over the town and the
surrounding landscape draws a contrast between the expanse of
the hills and the 'fat blot' of the town, which is cramped, 'a huddled
place full of chimneys and little shops with no gardens' and 'not
very tempting' (p. 6). Jeanette is identified as being working class –
'from the street' – and fights with middle-class, 'posh' children
'from the Avenue' (p. 6). Her house is small (it has one bedroom)
and her mother is building a bathroom. However, unlike May
and Mrs Arkwright, Jeanette and her mother do not speak in
regional dialect and accent, and her mother's class prejudice is
obvious at many points – her attitude to Maxi Ball's and sense of
superiority over the people who shop there being just one example.
Indeed, there are hints in this chapter that her mother had a
middle-class upbringing – she can play the piano and speak French,
unusual accomplishments for a working-class woman in the first
half of the twentieth century. Similarly, in the allegorical fairy tale
that tells of her conversion to Christianity, she is depicted as a
princess with an exciting and comfortable life. Later (in 'Exodus')
we learn of the impact that her own family's middle-class prejudice
had on her life when they disowned her for marrying a working-
class (gambling) man. This is possibly another factor explaining
why Jeanette's father 'was never quite good enough' (p. 11).

The use of first person narration and humour are effective in
undermining the authority of the church and in endearing us to
Jeanette (see Part 3, pp. 63–4, 70). The child Jeanette's innocent
misunderstandings and naïve perspective are a source of humour,
as when she interprets the 'unnatural passions' the women in the
paper shop are said to deal in as 'chemicals in their sweets' (p. 7).
However, we are also aware that the story is related by the knowing

voice of the older narrator, who comments **ironically** on these events. Humour is also used to ridicule the extremism of this church's views and the power with which its teachings are asserted (see Part 3, p. 70). At the banquet, the demon-obsessed Pastor Finch suggests that Jeanette, though she looks innocent, could potentially be 'a house of demons'. This terrifying experience for the child is deflated by the adult narrator's humorous belittling of the pastor's authority. He is presented as a ridiculous and repulsive figure, with his **melodramatic rhetoric** and his clammy hand, which he wipes on his trousers. Asides about the flying sandwich, Mrs Rothwell's deafness and her interruptions, and his wife's concern about him getting over-excited in this impromptu sermon all work to comically undermine his authority (p. 11). His assertion of the real and true versions of the stories when he takes over from Jeanette in playing with the Fuzzy Felt mocks his authority still further.

The lack of respect that we are encouraged to feel for the members of this church is important later when Jeanette puts the unorthodox tendencies that she shows here into action. Although she pretends childlike confusion over her rewrites of the biblical stories, we know that she wilfully mixes the stories up and that she seeks to create an alternative version or interpretation of the biblical stories for her own childishly sadistic pleasure. Her will to create alternative narratives in Fuzzy Felt here becomes a far more serious challenge to church doctrine when she interprets the Bible to accommodate her own desires and seeks to live out an alternative story to the missionary life her mother has planned for her. In the eyes of the church she does become 'a house of demons' and the violence implicit at the banquet (in the pastor's words, tone and actions) **foreshadows** the coming conflict and the treatment the supposedly demon-filled Jeanette will later receive.

Beeton, Mrs Isabella Beeton (1836–65) wrote a cookery book, the first to set out recipes in a formalised way; it also contained information on etiquette, management of home and servants, and organising dinner parties

Gwynn, Nell famous actress (1650–87), renowned for playing vivacious and comic roles, and a favourite in London society; from 1669 onwards she was the mistress of King Charles II and bore him two sons. As a child, she sold oranges outside the Drury Lane Theatre in London

Genesis first book of the Old Testament, which deals with the creation of the world, the Fall, the Noah story and the Tower of Babel; describes events in the lives of Abraham, Isaac, Lot, Jacob and Joseph

Virgin Mary in the New Testament, the pure and virginal mother of Jesus, who subsequently married Joseph and had other children; Christian saint beloved for her purity, patience and sympathy for human suffering – an ironic parallel to draw with Jeanette's mother

Sacrificial Lamb lambs were the most common Jewish sacrifice; refers by analogy to Jesus

Bonaparte, Napoleon French general (1769–1821), who led the French army during the Napoleonic Wars (1800–15); crowned himself Emperor of France (1804), but was forced to abdicate (1814); he briefly returned to lead the French army, a period known as the 'Hundred Days', but was defeated at Waterloo in 1816 and banished to the remote island of St Helena

Paschal Lamb the lamb sacrificed and eaten at the Jewish Passover; by analogy, the lamb is Jesus

Vengeance is mine saith the Lord Romans (12:19): 'Vengeance is mine; I will repay, saith the Lord'

Reeves, Jim US country singer (1923–64); specialised in syrupy love songs and songs with religious overtones

Jesus on the pinnacle the period of forty days when Jesus was in the wilderness and tempted by the Devil (Matthew 4:8–9 and Luke 4:5–7)

Mills and Boon main British publisher of popular romantic fiction

Flynn, Errol Hollywood actor (1909–59), born in Tasmania; reached the peak of his fame in the 1930s playing heroic roles

Heathen those who do not belong to a main religious group (Christian, Jewish or Muslim); in this book 'heathen' often refers to those who do not belong to Jeanette's mother's church

Blake, William poet and engraver (1757–1827), who had a mystic vision; considered gifted but insane until reappraisal began in the mid-nineteenth century; he was part of a progressive intellectual circle which diverged from Enlightenment poetic conventions and philosophical perspectives, and from limited Puritanical interpretations of Christianity

Hamlet eponymous hero of the Shakespearean tragedy, which revolves around power, family trauma, madness, lost love, deception and betrayal

Her flesh now, sprung from her head allusion to the Greek god Zeus, who overthrew his father in order to seize control of the universe; informed by the earth goddess Gaia that the child his wife was expecting would replace him as ruler, he swallowed his wife and the unborn baby. Eventually, Athena emerged from his head as a fully grown, fully armed warrior maiden; the virgin goddess of war, she took part in battles alongside male warriors. Suggests Jeanette's mother's megalomania and Jeanette's transgression of sex-gender norms

Moses Receiving the Ten Commandments the main Old Testament prophet, and leader and liberator of the Israelites; after forty years of wandering through the Sinai Desert, God delivered the Ten Commandments to Moses on Mount Sinai (Genesis 12:7); Moses did not reach the Promised Land, but glimpsed it before his death. Elsie is in many ways a Moses figure

Seven seals 'Then I saw in the right hand of the One who sat on the throne a scroll, with writing inside and out, and it was sealed up with seven seals' (Revelation 5:2–5)

Daniel in the lions' den 'Then the King commanded, that they brought Daniel, and cast him into the den of the lions' (Daniel 6:16); a Jew who retained his faith during captivity under the Babylonian kings Nebuchadnezzar, Belshazzar and Darius. He was locked inside a den of lions, but God prevented the lions from killing him; the story teaches faith in the face of extreme danger

Jonah and the whale minor Jewish prophet who refused to preach to the Ninevites; blamed for causing a storm on his sea journey, he was thrown overboard and swallowed by a large fish, traditionally a whale; three days later he was expelled and went to preach successfully in Nineveh

Nebuchadnezzaar Babylonian king (605–562 BC); destroyed the temple at Jerusalem and brought the Jewish people into captivity in Babylon. Set up a golden idol in Babylon and commanded that all should worship it. His punishment for his arrogance was insanity

Wise Men the three Magi, who travelled to Bethlehem to offer gifts to the baby Jesus

not seen hide nor hair not seen a glimpse

'ousie, 'ousie bingo call ('house') that signals a card is complete and therefore a winner

nipper child
Cash, Johnny country singer born 1932 in Arkansas, USA; reached the peak of his fame in the late 1960s
The Plain Truth Christian pamphlet
Elijah biblical figure who went to heaven without dying
Iron Curtain term formerly used to describe the separation of some Eastern European countries from the rest of Europe

EXODUS   Jeanette goes to school, recalls her operation and her growing friendship with Elsie; more about her mother's past is revealed

The chapter opens with her mother's irritation and agitation about Jeanette going to school. The narrative turns to Jeanette's memory of being temporarily deaf, a condition diagnosed by the church as a state of rapture. In another anecdotal digression, Elsie Norris is introduced. The story of Jeanette's deafness is resumed, with Miss Jewsbury's intervention ensuring that Jeanette gets medical attention. Jeanette is distressed when she is left alone at the hospital with only an orange for comfort, while her mother goes to collect Jeanette's pyjamas. Her mother returns later and Jeanette is taken to the children's ward, where she considers the animal images to be 'horrid'. Her mother writes a letter explaining that Jeanette will have an operation the following day, but offers no comfort and leaves Jeanette feeling abandoned and terrified.

Although Jeanette has her operation on Tuesday, her mother does not visit until the weekend because (ridiculously) she is waiting for the plumber to check her work in the bathroom. Similarly, she is busy elsewhere when Jeanette is discharged from hospital. Both these instances of maternal neglect are compensated for by Elsie Norris, who remains an important (mother) figure in Jeanette's life (see Part 3, pp. 54–5). Elsie visits Jeanette in hospital, and entertains and comforts her, telling her stories and jokes to amuse her, introducing her to some of her favourite poets and reciting poems, and making plans for when Jeanette is better. When Jeanette goes to stay with Elsie after her week in hospital, Elsie gives her a gift of three white mice in a cage made into a model of the fiery furnace.

Jeanette learns many things from Elsie, and although she is bewildered by some of Elsie's more philosophical statements, she is even more confused at school. In fact, after almost a year at school, Jeanette is finding things even 'more complex' than ever. At first she tries to fit in, but it is immediately apparent that her experience, centred on the church, and her religious frames of reference are severely at odds with those of the other children and teachers. Everyone finds her difference, her intelligence and her confidence in being right challenging and alarming. She is ostracised by the pupils and teachers alike, none of whom try to see things from her point of view or sympathise with the difficulty of her situation. Jeanette perseveres with trying to be 'ordinary' but all her attempts at achieving success – her sampler, her hyacinths, her painted Easter egg model and other creations – all meet with reproof. Tired of being bullied, Jeanette falls back on her imagination and her sadistic streak as protection, taunting the other children with stories of hell and demons. This leads the head teacher, Mrs Vole, to write a letter of complaint to her mother. Her mother's response is one of gleeful triumph at Jeanette's state of conflict with the 'Breeding Ground', and her assertion that the faithful are 'called to be apart' (p. 42) is unhelpful. She too demonstrates a total lack of sympathy for Jeanette's isolated and profoundly unhappy situation.

Jeanette's school experience makes her long for the sense of belonging she anticipates feeling at missionary school. Her only comfort at the end of her first school year is to think of the church's summer camp in Devon. Pastor Spratt's great missionary success is recalled and the military-style organisation and manipulative methods of converting people to the faith are mocked. Jeanette also recalls her mother's nostalgic memories of establishing their own gospel hall and her fundraising efforts, which earned her the name 'Jesus Belle'. More aspects of Jeanette's mother's past are revealed; she was attractive and had a number of 'old flames'. Her marriage, however, caused a rift with her family. The photograph of the woman in the 'Old Flames' section of the photograph album, said to be 'Eddy's sister', also hints that she too may have had a lesbian relationship.

Despite the fact that her efforts at school are continually thwarted, Jeanette does not despair. She survives the conflict and confusion of the secular world by reinterpreting and 'rearranging' information she is given so that it makes sense to her. She tries to cope with the sense of contradiction she feels by making up a story, which figures the geometrical shapes of the tetrahedron and the isosceles triangle as characters. What this story illustrates is that change is inevitable, nothing is ever absolutely fixed, and 'no emotion is the final one' (p. 48).

This final point is an important one in this chapter and in the novel as a whole. It is a counter and a challenge to Jeanette's mother's absolutist faith and marks the important first stages in Jeanette's questioning of and divergence from her mother's narrow-minded perspective on the world. What Jeanette learns from Elsie and from her clashes with the secular world causes her to see the importance of relativity. Realising that her mother and the church are wrong about the reason for her deafness marks a turning point, as Jeanette becomes aware that the church is not so stable or so absolutely right as she had thought. Jeanette's unconscious questioning and challenge to her mother's dogmatic views is also suggested through the **imagery** of fruit. In silent answer to the phrase that sums up her mother's limited and dogmatic outlook, 'Oranges are the only fruit', Jeanette suggests a range of fruit combinations. This comic undermining of her mother's world view hints at Jeanette's contrary view, which will emerge more fully later, and **foreshadows** Jeanette's more deliberate dissension from her mother's beliefs.

Jeanette's confrontation with the world outside her church family is presented in biblical terms. Like the Israelites leaving Egypt, as described in the Book of Exodus, Jeanette leaves the shelter of home and goes out into the wilderness of school. Like them, Jeanette is guided by a pillar of cloud (the unwritten rules of school) which she is unable to interpret. In this chapter the church and the secular world of school are represented as being opposites; the events in both spheres are **juxtaposed** to show the distance between two aspects of Jeanette's life – school and church. However, although she is a success in one sphere and a failure in another, both institutions, in effect, fail her;

in both she is neglected, her views are ignored and her needs unmet.

As in the first chapter, the adult narrator's voice comments cynically and **ironically** on events and undermines the authorities who so consistently misunderstand the child and treat her unfairly. Seen through the young Jeanette's eyes, this treatment invites the reader's sympathy for her situation, and the older, more judgemental narrative voice encourages a critical attitude to the majority of adults Jeanette encounters. Although Jeanette is in a powerless position, the use of humour creates a sense of her as feisty and resourceful, imaginative and determined; she may be young and vulnerable, but her typically childish humour suggests that she is not cowed by authority and asserts her views.

There is an overall sense of moving forward in time as Jeanette gets older in this chapter, but the narrative is also very anecdotal and digressive. Subjects are discussed, dropped and then picked up again a few paragraphs or pages later, and the intimate tone gives the narrative a conversational feel. The lack of a clear, linear development in this chapter could also suggest the confusion that Jeanette feels at this point in her life.

Exodus second book of the Old Testament; deals with the departure of the Israelites from Egypt, led by Moses

Glorious Things of Thee Are Spoken hymn of praise written by John Newton (1725–1807):'Glorious things of Thee are spoken, / Zion, city of our God'

Lead Kindly Light hymn of personal petition to God, written by Cardinal John Henry Newman (1801–90); Lead, Kindly Light, amid the encircling gloom, / Lead Thou me on! / The night is dark, and I am far from home – / Lead Thou me on!'

Noah's Ark Noah was a biblical patriarch whom God ordered to build an ark in order to save one male and one female of every species from the oncoming destruction of the Flood; when the flood waters subsided, the Earth could be replenished (Genesis 6)

Jane Eyre eponymous heroine in novel with proto-feminist elements by Charlotte Brontë (1816–55), which caused a scandal when first published; Jane is a governess, who falls in love with her employer, Mr Rochester; however, on the day of their wedding he is revealed as a bigamist, his first wife being alive but insane and locked in the attic; Jane's cousin, St John Rivers, asks her to marry him so that she can help him fulfil his ambition to be a missionary in India; Jane has a choice between acting on her passion and marrying Rochester, or following her Christian duty and marrying St John; she chooses Rochester, whose first wife dies in a fire. Jeanette has a similar choice

Great War World War I (1914–18)

Swinburne, Algernon Charles poet (1837–1909) associated with the Pre-Raphaelite circle; his poems caused moral outcry because of their preoccupation with the Marquis de Sade, masochism and *femmes fatales*, also because of his outspoken repudiation of Christianity, his hatred of authority (which owes much to Blake) and his heavy drinking. He was also a perceptive and original critic

Goblin Market long poem by Christina Rossetti (1830–94), poet and devout High Anglican, sister of painter Dante Gabriel Rossetti; the poem is a cautionary tale about the dangers of succumbing to the sexual power of men; it is also suggestively homoerotic

Yeats, W.B. (William Butler) Irish poet (1865–1939) interested in Irish lore and legends, Irish traditions and nationalist themes, and mystic religion and the supernatural; senator of the Irish Free State (1922–8) and winner of the Nobel Prize for literature in 1923

All things fall and are built again / And those that build them again are gay from 'Lapis Lazuli' by W.B. Yeats, in *Last Poems* (1939)

Prince Albert German prince (1819–61), husband of Queen Victoria; he encouraged the arts, as well as social and industrial reforms

Shadrach, Meshach and Abednego in the fiery furnace figures of the Old Testament who refused to worship the golden idol and were thrown into the fiery furnace by King Nebuchadnezzar (p. 16); miraculously, they were rescued by God (Daniel 3). Allusions to the fiery furnace suggest a punishment that harms those who attempt to enforce it

Pentecost the beginning of the Christian Church with the bestowing of the holy spirit on the apostles

Nightingale, Florence nursing pioneer (1820–1910), who tended the injured during the Crimean War, establishing better standards of care than previously available; she became a popular heroine and spent the rest of her life campaigning for improving public health and for a trained nursing service

Clive of India Robert Clive of Plassey (1725–74), British soldier and administrator, who joined the East India Company, defeated a large Indian force at the battle of Plassey in 1757 and reformed the Civil Service in Calcutta

Palmerston, Henry John Temple, 3rd Viscount British politician (1784–1865), acted as foreign secretary and prime minister

Newton, Sir Isaac famous mathematician (1624–1727), who invented the reflecting telescope, among other things, and discovered the laws affecting the movements of planets

An army marches on its stomach attributed to Napoleon Bonaparte (see p. 15)

Suffer little children from Matthew (19:14): 'Suffer little children to come unto me, and forbid them not: for such is the kingdom of heaven'; Jesus insisted that children be brought to him for blessing

Jeremiah one of the great prophets of the Old Testament; he lived during the Babylonian conquest of Jerusalem. Following the destruction of the temple, he put the emphasis on the individual rather than the nation and saw the source of religion as lying in the human heart

The Ten Commandments film directed by Cecil B. DeMille (1956), starring Charlton Heston, Yul Brynner and Anne Baxter

Reynolds, Sir Joshua leading English portrait painter (1723–92); first president of the Royal Academy in 1768

Turner, Joseph Mallord William English landscape painter (1775–1851), considered one of the most original artists of his day; popularly renowned for his paintings flooded with hazy light. He is buried next to Sir Joshua Reynolds in St Paul's Cathedral

Wordsworth, William English poet (1770–1850); his love of nature is reflected in his poems

The Annunciation the Angel of the Lord informs the Virgin Mary of her immaculate conception

Pre-Raphaelite the Pre-Raphaelite Brotherhood (1848–53) was a group of British painters who aimed to revitalise art by emulating the work of Italian artists before the time of Raphael (1483–1520); they had a fascination for the dream world and medieval settings, and took literary and biblical figures and scenes as their subjects; group members included Dante Gabriel Rossetti, John Everett Millais and Holman Hunt

Morris, Janey wife of the painter, poet and designer William Morris (1834–96) and one of Dante Gabriel Rossetti's models

Coleridge and the Man from Porlock in the introductory note to the poem 'Kubla Khan' by Samuel Taylor Coleridge (1772–1834) it is suggested that the poet's visionary state was interrupted while writing the poem: 'At this moment he was unfortunately called out by a person from Porlock' – with the result that the poem ends abruptly

Wagner, Richard German composer and conductor (1813–83); themes of redemption and renunciation are preoccupations in his work. His opera *Parsifal*, completed in 1882, draws on myths and various versions of the Holy Grail legend, and explores ideas about belief, human structures and feminine psychology

Brunhilda confronts her father...Wodin Brunhilda is the princess beloved by the hero Sigurd in Wagner's *Ring of the Nibelungs*; in the Teutonic myth on which Wagner draws, she is one of the Valkyries (maiden warriors). Wodin is the Scandinavian god of wisdom, poetry, war and culture

A Streetcar Named Desire film directed by Elia Kazan (1951), based on a play of the same name by American dramatist Tennessee Williams; stars Vivien Leigh and Marlon Brando

Now Voyager romantic film directed by Irving Rapper (1942); stars Bette Davis and Paul Henreid

Tell, William fourteenth-century hero of Swiss legend and a universal symbol of resistance to oppression

Ford, Henry American industrialist (1863–1947), who established assembly line production to mass-produce cars. He was a social pioneer, introducing the eight-hour day to his Ford Motor Company in 1914, and offering a minimum wage and profit-sharing scheme to his workers

Chrysler Building New York skyscraper built in Art Deco style (1928–30); with seventy-seven storeys, it was the world's tallest building, until overtaken by the Empire State

King Canute forcing back the waves Canute (*c*.995–1035) was a Danish king who ruled England (1019–35), maintaining peace throughout his reign. Legend has it that he demonstrated the limitations of his powers to sycophantic courtiers by failing to halt the incoming waves

Tower of Babel a tower built in Babylonia in an attempt to reach heaven; it is seen as a symbol of human arrogance. The building was halted when God made the builders speak in different languages so that they could not understand one another (Genesis 2:1–9)

When the children of Israel...night the journey of the Israelites from Egypt to the Promised Land (Exodus 13:20–1)

LEVITICUS   Jeanette recalls the incident of Next Door 'fornicating'; her mother's successful role in the church is described; Jeanette's theological disagreement is introduced

Jeanette recalls an example of her mother's 'methods' for dealing with the behaviour of her neighbours, whom she considers to be 'Heathen'. When they return from Communion one Sunday, Jeanette's mother and Mrs White are scandalised when they realise that the neighbours are 'fornicating', and hurriedly send Jeanette out to buy ice-creams. When Jeanette returns, they sing a rousing Victorian hymn, 'Ask the Saviour to Help You', in order to quell the sinful activities of Next Door. This prompts an angry response from the neighbours, who shout over the wall that divides their yards. Jeanette's mother answers with what is a cruelly apt quotation from the Bible. Feeling victorious after this confrontation, she returns inside smiling and ready to cook Sunday dinner.

Jeanette's mother is a powerful figure in their church community and has created a role for herself as a 'missionary on the home front' (p. 53), a role she equates with the heroically depicted and high-profile missionary work of Pastor Spratt. Her shrewd business sense and talents for promotion and marketing are important to her role as treasurer for the Society of the Lost. Jeanette recalls spending a weekend at the society's guest house for the bereaved in Morecambe at the 'busy season' for conversions (just before Easter when 'malingering illnesses' prompt people to adopt a faith in fear of imminent death, p. 55). Jeanette helps her mother's friend, who is not named, to make wreaths after her floristry business is given a boost by an epidemic at a local boarding school. The narrative leaps forward and we are told that some years later Jeanette will work on Saturdays laying out the dead in the business her mother's friend establishes with an undertaker.

During the society's 'special conference', a sermon on perfection prompts another significant turning point for Jeanette in terms of her doubts about church doctrine. Her first theological disagreement is related in terms of a fairy tale about a prince who seeks a wife who is perfect. His definition of perfection is flawlessness (which parallels the views of Jeanette's mother and the church) and this is impossible to attain. The definition of perfection that the wise woman offers is informed by her understanding of physics and older forms of wisdom, such as myths and astrology. In her definition perfection is a relative, not a fixed, value or quality and is achieved through balance and harmony; finding personal balance is the key to finding perfection.

As in Genesis, this fairy tale functions to develop an aspect of the realist narrative and to represent the process of Jeanette growing up and having her own opinions. The reason that Jeanette's disagreement with her church's beliefs is expressed in a fairy tale could be because it is too painful for her to question the foundations of her faith in a realist way. Alternatively, it could be that Jeanette finds it impossible to question the authority of the church and her mother other than in a fantasy mode. There are at least two levels on which this fairy tale can be understood: as a feminist revision of the gender politics of traditional fairy tales, and as an **allegory** for elements of the realist narrative. Like typical fairy tales, it is concerned with a prince's quest for a perfect wife, and it is structured in groups of three – three events, attributes, sections of the prince's book. However, the usual romantic pattern is comically undercut; the most beautiful woman is business-like, bold, intelligent, outspoken and fiercely independent, and the love plot collapses when she refuses to marry the prince and live, as the courtiers hope and as readers might expect, 'happily ever after' (p. 62). The class prejudice of traditional fairy tales is also subtly exposed; in this tale, attaining royal status is not something to be aspired to, and the humour of the tale is at the expense of class privilege: 'The prince himself had lost the use of his legs from sitting still so long' (p. 61).

However, the fairy tale also explores the tensions between Jeanette and her mother which are not fully expressed, or not fully realised (by the child Jeanette) in the realist narrative. The prince represents her mother's extreme and unbalanced views (she is 'mad' in Mrs Arkwright's opinion) and his advisors correspond to the congregation. Like her fellow church members, his subjects consider him to be 'good' and a 'valuable leader', and he is described as 'pretty'; like her he is 'petulant' and volatile, punishing those who disagree with him (the goose, for example, p. 60). His subjects respond hysterically when they feel that his, and therefore their own, authority is threatened by the woman's alternative views, and the prince himself is somewhat fascistic in his desire for a 'perfect race' (p. 60).

The fairy tale suggests the sense of threat Jeanette feels about openly questioning the church's doctrine; the goose and the wise woman, who are both killed for challenging the opinion of the prince and his court, act as two cautionary figures. This fairy tale also **foreshadows** events; Jeanette does not get her head cut off, but is cut off from her mother and the church when she challenges their theological views later. The tale, like some of the other fairy tales in the novel, does, however, also explore the affection and sympathy Jeanette feels for her mother, despite her mother's actions. In this tale the prince learns humility from the wise woman when he accepts that he is wrong. However, his advisors perceive this as a threat to his power and authority and to the existing social (**patriarchal**) order, and persuade him to reject what he has learned and to punish the woman for her 'evil'. The need to adhere to protocol and a perceived threat to the existing order prompts the prince's betrayal and this foreshadows later events when Jeanette's mother similarly betrays Jeanette. The end of the fairy tale ridicules the prince's ongoing quest for perfection in its reference to Frankenstein's monster – a creature, especially in Boris Karloff's portrayal in the 1931 film, far from perfect. It suggests that such an extreme adherence to a single and narrow doctrine will result in something grotesque.

Again, the church members are held up to ridicule in this chapter, and the technique of using Jeanette's childlike innocence to comment humorously on the actions of the congregation is effective in exposing their hypocrisy and mocking their self-righteousness and intolerance. Mrs White is a key target for ridicule in this chapter (see Part 3, p. 58) and once again Jeanette's childlike logic (that sins are usually performed quietly to avoid detection) subtly undermines the narrow-minded views of the church, here the view that sex is a sin. The events recalled in this chapter testify to Jeanette's mother's furious intolerance and the fierce vindictiveness with which she asserts her views. Her powerful passion leads her to unorthodox expressions of her beliefs – she 'wrought her own huge chords' which, like her, are overpowering and all-encompassing: 'No note was exempt' (p. 53). She has a strong sense of her own authority, and is absolutely certain that she is right.

Given this context, we are able to fully appreciate the trepidation with which Jeanette tests out her disagreement with her mother's doctrine. The adult narrator also provides many instances of **irony**, which undercut her mother's powerful views. For example, the juxtaposition of her mother's promotion to the role of treasurer for the Society for the Lost, presumably an organisation offering sympathy and comfort to those in distress, with her callous response to Pierre's threat of suicide is ironic. It highlights the gap between the public role she is forging for herself and reality which contradicts this. Similarly, Jeanette's mother and Mrs White sing 'Yield Not to Temptation', yet Jeanette's mother's success in increasing the number of subscriptions to the Society for the Lost is a result of 'tempting offers' and her creation of exclusive gifts.

Leviticus third book of the Old Testament, which contains the fundamentals of Jewish law and religious ceremonial following the rebuilding of the temple c.516 BC

fornication sexual relations between unmarried people

The Lord will smite you with the boils of Egypt reference to one of the ten plagues that affected the Egyptians (Exodus 7–12)

Second Coming the belief that Christ would return during the lifetime of those alive when he was crucified

Rechabite member of Rechab, a biblical tribe

Holy Grail in medieval legend this is the bowl that Jesus used at the Last Supper, brought to Britain by Joseph of Arimathea; it became a symbol of perfection sought by many knights

Mount Carmel a high ridge in northern Palestine, the scene of a contest between Elijah and the prophets of Baal; it has become the home of the Carmelite order

> **St Teresa of Avila** Spanish Carmelite nun and mystic (1515–82), who took a
> long time to become converted to a life of perfection; wrote *The Way of
> Perfection, Foundations* and *The Interior Castle*
> **The importance of being earnest** literary joke; refers to Oscar Wilde's play of
> the same title, which is in part a mockery of Victorian society; Wilde was
> tried and imprisoned for homosexuality in 1892
> **Libra...Pisces** signs of the zodiac, which represent balance
> **this geezer gets a bolt through the neck** reference to the first film made of
> Mary Shelley's novel *Frankenstein*, directed by James Whale in 1931; Boris
> Karloff's memorable portrayal of the creature has become the iconic
> representation of the monster. The novel, written in 1818, describes Victor
> Frankenstein's experiment to create life, which ends in disaster. The novel
> raises issues of hubris (excessive pride), usurping God's role as creator, and
> poor parenting – Victor abandons his 'child', the creature

NUMBERS   **Before the development of her lesbian relationship with
Melanie, Jeanette struggles to understand marriage;
Melanie joins the church, but the girls' sense of security
is soon shattered**

Jeanette's struggles to understand the confusing information she receives
about heterosexual relationships and about being female are comically
presented. She has a recurring nightmare about getting married, takes
literally her neighbour's statement that she married a pig, and challenges
the idea that girls are by definition 'sweet'. She looks to books for the
solution to the contradiction she perceives between what she is told about
relationships (the ideal) and what she knows from observing the reality.
The fairy tales in the library only reinforce her anxieties, and she
comically concludes that there is 'a terrible conspiracy' that tricks women
into marrying beasts on the false pretext that they will turn into princes
(p. 71). Questioning her aunty about men being beasts only confirms
Jeanette's suspicions about marriage being a disappointing experience for
women. Jeanette's mother evades her daughter's anxieties and curiosity
about her marriage, diverting Jeanette's attention to the missionary life
she has planned for her. However, Jeanette is now aware that her
mother's explanations cannot be entirely trusted and reveals the two
shocking moments of discovering that her mother has misled her – one

is her re-telling of *Jane Eyre* and the other is her silence about the fact that Jeanette is adopted.

Jeanette seeks alternative sources of information, but is only more confused by the conversation she hears when eavesdropping on Doreen and Betty by hiding in a dustbin. She hears of husbands who are useless, unfaithful and violent, and again of how women's illusions about marriage are shattered by the reality. However, marriage is also seen to be compulsory, and the stigma attached to lesbianism is a powerful deterrent to acting differently. Doreen's daughter, Jane, could break free from this situation and go to university, but the women, despite criticising their husbands, still defer to men and allow them to dictate the future of their daughters.

Jeanette consoles herself with the prospect of becoming a missionary and leaves love to chance. The narrative leaps forward to one Saturday when Jeanette is fourteen and meets Melanie, with whom she falls in love – her first such experience. Jeanette is now more argumentative and tries to resist her mother's selfishly motivated insistence that Jeanette go with her to town. They travel on the bus with Ida (one of the paper shop women said to be lesbians) and May. At the butcher's Jeanette tears the sleeve off her mackintosh and embarrasses her mother by retorting angrily to Mrs Clifton's interfering comments. Despite Jeanette's protests, her mother buys her a bright pink mac from the seconds shop, which is too large. At the fish stall she meets Melanie, who works there, but is hurried off to Trickett's snack bar, where her mother has arranged to meet May and Ida. Betty, who works at the café, criticises Mrs Clifton's middle-class snobbery, and Jeanette's mother is clearly confused and distressed about her own class allegiance. Jeanette is offered a Saturday job and is happy because she can think about and watch Melanie every Saturday. One day Melanie is not at the fish stall, and Jeanette's sense of shock sends her into a comic reverie about whelks. Just as she is about to despair at her loss, she meets Melanie, who now has a job at the library. Jeanette tells Melanie about her church and the following day Melanie attends the Sunday service. Pastor Finch, on his regional tour, gives a sermon on the 'epidemic of demons' and unnatural passions sweeping the north-west. Melanie confesses her sins and is 'saved' in the pastor's old Bedford van, cunningly converted into a salvation bus (p. 83). She asks Jeanette to

be her religious counsellor and Jeanette goes to her house every
Monday.

Despite the fact that Jeanette talks often about Melanie at home,
her mother thinks that she is in love with another new convert called
Graham. She decides it's time to tell Jeanette the cautionary tale of her
mistake in thinking the symptoms of a stomach ulcer were those of being
in love. That evening Jeanette goes to Melanie's house and is asked to
stay the night (just as old flame Pierre asked her mother). Their
relationship becomes a sexual one and afterwards they are together as
much as possible. Although they fear their feelings might be 'Unnatural
Passions', they conclude that this isn't possible because their feelings are
good. They work together to organise the Harvest Festival Banquet and
feel safe within their church family.

> The brief **allegorical** tale that ends this chapter warns, however,
> that the safety they feel may soon be threatened. Although they feel
> wholly secure about belonging to the church, and happy and
> fulfilled in their relationship, which is so bound up with their faith,
> the **dramatic irony** that is brought to the fore at the end of this
> chapter creates a strong sense of discomfort at the inevitable
> reaction of the church. The effect is that of a 'time bomb' as, with
> mounting tension, the shattering of Jeanette and Melanie's
> innocence and happiness is anticipated (see Part 4, pp. 81, 83–4).

> Throughout the chapter there is an increasing sense of women's
> disappointment and disillusionment with marriage and men.
> Marriage restricts the fulfilment of women's desires and ambitions,
> yet is the only acceptable option. The dominant heterosexual norms
> are challenged and criticised via the exposure of heterosexual
> romance myths that pervade Western culture (in the form of fairy
> tales) as lies and tricks. This negative depiction of marriage and
> heterosexual relationships in the first part of the chapter, along with
> the presence of Ida, and Pastor Finch's sermon about demons and
> unnatural passions, prepares the reader for Jeanette's first lesbian
> relationship.

> **Numbers** fourth book of the Old Testament, which records the wanderings of
> the Israelites through the desert wilderness to the Promised Land; Moses
> appears as a prophet who speaks directly to God

Jane Eyre novel by Charlotte Brontë (see p. 20)
The Man in the Iron Mask film directed by James Whale (1939), starring Louis Haywood and Joan Bennett; based on a novel by Alexandre Dumas (1802–70)
Keats, John English Romantic poet and surgeon (1795–1821); he gave up medicine to devote himself to poetry
And it was evening and it was morning; another day echoes Genesis (1:13) and suggests new birth
Winter Palace home of the Russian royal family, stormed in 1917 during the revolution; discovering a huge wine cellar, the rebels got drunk and chaos erupted

DEUTERONOMY   **A philosophical reflection on the nature of history, fiction, truth and understanding**

In this densely packed and highly **allusive** chapter we are offered a philosophical reflection on history and storytelling. The status of history as a factual, objective, realistic and undeniably true reporting of the past is questioned, and the dichotomy between history (fact) and storytelling (fiction) is disrupted. History is only a number of events made to form a cohesive narrative. It is a way of organising, ordering and shaping the multiplicity of past events (a 'string full of knots', p. 91) into a single chain of events that we can grasp. Inevitably, history is selective; certain events only become historical fact through a process of eliminating other events. The **metaphorical** squeezing of 'this oozing world between [the] two boards and typeset' (p. 93) of a history book involves many omissions, so 'history is a means of denying the past', or many aspects of it (p. 92). As the references to empire, economics and Pol Pot suggest, these omissions are not arbitrary; we might think that history is objective and neutral, but this is not the case. The selection of events reported as history is **ideologically** motivated and determined; it reinforces the dominant cultural views and endorses existing power structures.

For instance, the argument in this chapter seems to suggest that the often unquestioned perspective offered by history fuelled the drive to build an empire (whether this is specifically the British Empire is not clear, but the same argument can apply to any other expansionist developments, or empire building). History is powerful in manipulating the way individuals and nations perceive the world and their role in it. Winterson seems to be suggesting that historical narratives can cause nations to be complicit with specific, ideologically determined views – for instance, the belief in European supremacy and the necessity of imposing Western values on to other peoples (in order to 'civilise' them). Pol Pot's elimination of history is an extreme example of a lack of objectivity in dealing with and constructing history. It also highlights the way that power can be exerted through control of what can count as history. Since history, like stories, is about the formation of identity, it has a powerful impact on our sense of our selves as individuals and as part of a community or nation.

The construction of history is also said to be economically motivated and closely linked with capitalist enterprise, from the production of history books to the exploitation of natural resources in other countries. For instance, early explorations that were considered 'crazy' are reinterpreted and revalued in light of the material benefits they have brought as time has gone on, 'potatoes or tobacco or, best of all, gold' (p. 93).

However, while the rigidity and fixed nature of history can offer only a fallacious sense of order and security, stories can offer both order and balance. Humorously, drawing an analogy between digestion and understanding, Winterson suggests that having control over what goes into the mind, just as we control what enters our digestive system, is much healthier than if we constantly 'eat out', not really knowing what we are absorbing. This means that if we accept the single version of events offered as history, our perception of the world is likely to be unhealthily restricted and blocked, and our ability to understand the world itself hindered. By contrast, the acceptance of a multiple view and tolerance for a variety of perspectives on and versions of events will enable everyone to make up their own minds, and to have control over the ingredients, 'what's going in'. The only way to be able to chew over events in an informed way is summed up in the final sentence: 'If you want to keep your own teeth, make your own sandwiches...' (p. 93).

This discussion of history and story, fact and fiction falls at the centre of the novel and at a crucial point in Jeanette's life. The security she feels in her relationship with Melanie and with their place in the church is about to be lost. The refusal to reduce events to a single interpretation, to restrict stories and make them fit into a specific organising frame of reference, is one way that Jeanette will be able to hold on to a positive sense of her identity in the face of the narrow-mined interpretation that the church will put on to it. The idea that understanding of the past can change with distance and hindsight is also significant to Jeanette's life, as from this point onward she begins to reassess her own past in the light of her present.

This discussion of history is part of the revisionary process going on in the novel as a whole. The traditional interpretation of the historical account that the Bible offers is questioned (later Jeanette uses the very words of the Bible in the defence of her sexuality), and Winterson rewrites its stories to reinstate omissions (of a diversity of sexual preferences), as she also subtly interweaves other references to lesbian and gay stories of the past into her novel (Oscar Wilde, Charlotte Brontë and Christina Rossetti, for instance). She is also offering a broader revision of history as a traditionally male-dominated enterprise; the events usually recorded as history – wars, politics, monarchy – are dominated by men and by patriarchal power structures, while women are generally excluded or marginalised.

Deuteronomy fifth book of the Old Testament; restates the Ten Commandments and records the final events in the life of Moses

Pol Pot Cambodian communist politician (1925–99) and tyrannical leader of the Khmer Rouge guerrilla organisation, which killed millions of innocent people

brave new world from Shakespeare's *The Tempest*; Miranda, daughter of the magician Prospero, has been brought up in isolation on an island; when she sees people on whom her father has practised his magic, she says, 'O brave new world / That has such people in't' (V:i).

Aldous Huxley (1894–1963) used the phrase ironically as the title for his dystopian novel (1932)

Atlantis legendary island of great beauty and wealth, overwhelmed by the sea

Pilgrim Fathers group of people who fled religious persecution in England; sailed to America in the *Mayflower* and founded a settlement at New Plymouth, Massachusetts, in 1620

El Dorado non-existent place in South America, rumoured to have abundant gold; early European explorers wreaked havoc among the native peoples in their search for it

St George patron saint of England

JOSHUA   **Jeanette and Melanie's relationship is condemned as sinful; Melanie repents and Jeanette is exorcised. Melanie leaves and Jeanette's life returns to 'normal' until Melanie visits during the Christmas vacation. Jeanette's repressed sexuality re-emerges and she begins a lesbian relationship with Katy. Melanie returns later with her fiancé**

Jeanette has told her mother some of what she feels for Melanie, but since then her mother has seemed preoccupied. On this particular Saturday, however, her mother's mood has become more cheerful and she and Mrs White have cleaned the house in preparation for some forthcoming event. When Mrs White evades Jeanette's questions about what this will be, she goes for a walk up the hill with their dog. As she gazes over the town, Jeanette reflects on her unusual feeling of uncertainty about her situation. This feeling and the location trigger a painful memory of her biological mother's visit to her home when she was younger. Jeanette does not make a conscious connection between what she has told her mother and her mother's preoccupied silence. However, without consciously knowing why, she does feel the need to be secretive about her nights with Melanie, and even more so since Elsie (with whom they often stay) is in hospital. Returning from her walk, Jeanette finds that her mother, unusually, has gone to stay with Mrs White, so Jeanette goes to spend the night with Melanie and they discuss their plans for the future.

The following day at church, Jeanette's feelings of security and utter happiness with Melanie and with her place in the church are shattered when the pastor accuses them of sin and condemns their relationship. Melanie repents immediately, but Jeanette protests this interpretation and, like the pastor, uses biblical authority to defend her view. She is in a state of shock, and after a night at Miss Jewsbury's house, Jeanette goes home to collect her school things but is caught by the group of church members who have been waiting to 'save' her. They pray over her for the whole day; she refuses to renounce Melanie so she is locked in the parlour with no light and no food for thirty-six hours. Jeanette becomes delirious, but when the pastor and the others return, she is calm, and cheerfully and quickly repents. She immediately goes to find Melanie at her relatives' house in Halifax, and they spend a final, distressing night together; both are emotionally shattered and confused by their experience.

Jeanette gets glandular fever, and while she is ill, her mother ransacks her room and burns all the written evidence of her relationship with Melanie. By the time Jeanette recovers, Melanie has gone away before she goes to university. With Melanie absent from her life, Jeanette slots back into her role in the church and, on a successful tent mission in Blackpool, meets and is attracted to a new convert called Katy. Back at home the year passes by, marked only by church festivals and celebrations. Katy attends church regularly, and she and Jeanette become close. It is only when Melanie comes home for a visit, however, that Jeanette's repressed feelings again surface, bringing with them a sense of fear and panic.

Despite Jeanette's discomfort and rebuffs, Melanie is keen to spend time with her. She watches the Nativity play, written by Jeanette's mother, visits Jeanette at home, holds a bunch of mistletoe as she listens to the carols the church members sing in the town, catches the same bus as Jeanette on the way home, and offers Jeanette an orange. Although the motivation for her actions is slightly ambiguous, Melanie seems to want only to be friends with Jeanette and appears unconscious of the temptations her actions represent for Jeanette. Melanie is 'serene', unlike Jeanette, who is in a state of turmoil. Jeanette attributes her distress to fear of her physical illness returning, but as this coincided with the trauma of her lesbianism being discovered and punished, the emotions associated with both are inextricably bound together.

Seeing that Jeanette is worried, Katy invites her to stay at her caravan for the weekend, and this begins their long-term relationship, which they keep secret from the church. Melanie returns at Easter the following year with her fiancé. Jeanette is jealous and bitter, and when Melanie's fiancé patronisingly pats her arm and says he forgives Jeanette and Melanie for their lesbian sin, Jeanette spits at him.

Focusing on Jeanette's adolescence, this chapter is concerned with the great changes she undergoes as she comes to accept her lesbian sexuality. Simultaneously, she becomes increasingly detached from her mother, both emotionally and in terms of her beliefs. Jeanette's experience here is a rite of passage, which marks the end of her childhood and results in irrevocable transformation.

Jeanette cannot fully account for her unusual feelings of uncertainty and apprehension, and the need she feels for secrecy about her relationship with Melanie. However, the parallels implicit in the memory of her only other moment of uncertainty – when her biological mother tried to see her – offer some clues to the reason for Jeanette's feelings. What she recalls of her adoptive mother's response – a refusal of Jeanette's wishes, a violent assertion of the centrality of her own role, and silence about what she perceived as a challenge to her authority and a defiance of her views – **foreshadows** the similarly extreme response that unfolds in this chapter. The series of unusual events that Jeanette notes but does not analyse also builds the reader's sense of discomfort. Her mother's lack of sympathy and support contributes to Jeanette's earlier sense of trauma, but in this chapter her mother's more active attempt to destroy a crucial part of Jeanette's life and identity (her participation in the exorcism and her burning of Melanie's letters) leads to an unbridgeable rift in the mother–daughter relationship. Both her earlier experience and the events related in this chapter mark points of irrevocable change in Jeanette's perception and understanding of her relationship with her mother.

The interspersing of Jeanette's dreams, hallucinations and the fantasy sections with the realist narrative is crucial to our understanding of the changes Jeanette experiences. These sections complement her experiences and form a narrative of the interior, which maps the subtle emotional and psychological changes taking place in her. They are **allegories** for the difficult and traumatic process Jeanette is unconsciously going through of coping with her fears about her situation and of reaching a decision about accepting her sexuality. The fantasy sections indirectly express the complex and contradictory feelings of anger, betrayal and loss that she has for her mother, feelings which are impossible for her to articulate explicitly. These non-realist sections also develop the themes of the novel – the risky quest for self-knowledge and identity, and the fear of exile, which is weighed in the balance with life-denying but safe options.

The orange demon that Jeanette hallucinates about while she is locked in the parlour is symbolic of her lesbian sexuality and of the important discovery she has made about herself. The conversation she has with it expresses the process by which she realises that the church's rigid views of good and evil cannot hold, and that being free of all sin is an impossibility. Jeanette realises at some level that her lesbian sexuality is an integral part of her. However, at this point she needs to act pragmatically and pretends to deny her lesbian demon. She represses her sexuality but it gradually surfaces, and, eventually, she consciously accepts her lesbian desires. Her dream of the City of Lost Chances expresses her fears about not attaining future happiness, of missing opportunities for fulfilment beyond the life she knows, as a result of denying her lesbian sexuality; she fears being emotionally and psychologically 'mutilated' (p. 108). The City of Lost Chances recurs in the allegory of the Forbidden City and is the place where those unwilling to give up security for the risky business of pursuing self-fulfilment and self-discovery find themselves.

This allegorical section follows the passage that describes Jeanette's mother's purging of all the evidence of Jeanette's relationship with Melanie, a betrayal that has a profound effect on Jeanette and leads to the final breach in their relationship. This fantasy section expresses not only the devastation Jeanette feels at this betrayal, but also the fact that, like Humpty Dumpty, Jeanette will never be the same. The use of a familiar nursery rhyme at this point is not an attempt to lighten the impact of this experience on Jeanette. On the contrary, it stresses the trauma of it by emphasising her vulnerability. It also marks the end of her childhood, when such rhymes can help children to come to terms with the inevitability of loss. The implication is that the rhymes are now insufficient to express the immensity of the loss she feels. Having said this, however, the trivial rhyme prompted by Jeanette's apparent realisation of her attraction to Katy – 'Katy sat in a deckchair and Katy looked at the sun./ Katy ate an ice-cream and Katy looked like fun' (p. 114) – serves to displace her anxiety about her repressed sexuality.

Walls, physical and **metaphorical**, figure significantly in this chapter. Their dual function of protecting and restricting becomes the crux of Jeanette's decision. The allegory of the Forbidden City suggests the painful choices Jeanette is presented with: either to stay within the security of the church and her family, choosing 'the wall' that will protect but also restrict her, or to go beyond what she knows, choosing to act on her desires and taking the risk of going unprotected into an uncertain future. At this point she chooses to remain within the physical walls of home and within the moral boundaries of the church. However, the distinction made between **physics** and **metaphysics** suggests how she tries to negotiate a path between the two stark choices of exile or self-denial. She uses the material walls of family and church to satisfy her physical needs, but conceptualises the more flexible boundary of a circle for her emotional and spiritual needs.

In the realist narrative, after her illness she seems to have decided to accept the church's moral boundaries, but she asserts her emotional and spiritual freedom in her increasing independence from her mother. At this point, Jeanette seems unsure about her sexuality; however, the orange demon's brief reappearance suggests that, although she does not consciously realise it, she has made an irrevocable decision to accept her lesbianism. The 'rough brown pebble' that the orange demon throws to her **symbolises** the choice that she has made. Jeanette's conscious acceptance that her lesbianism is an integral part of her identity is made clear by her decision to openly defend her choice regardless of her mother's response. The fact that the symbolic rough brown pebble becomes literalised, crossing over from the fantasy/psychological level to the realist level of narrative, reinforces the decision she has made (pp. 128, 133).

The allegory of the walled garden echoes and revises the biblical myth of the Garden of Eden in which Adam and Eve eat the forbidden fruit, thereby transgressing God's laws, and are expelled from paradise. It suggests that Jeanette has made the decision to repress her sexuality no longer. She has decided to metaphorically eat the fruit from the Tree of Knowledge, although she knows this will lead to her expulsion from the church. The suggestion that this exile may not be permanent, and that she might be able to enter the garden again one day, is an attempt to alleviate some of her fear at leaving what is known and secure.

The title of the chapter refers to the biblical story of the Battle of Jericho. Joshua's faith in God's promise and his trust in God's instruction to walk around the walls and to blow a trumpet leads to the fall of the city walls and victory for the righteous. The several battles in this chapter echo and revise this biblical myth; the battles include the church's battle to save Jeanette's soul, Jeanette's battle with the church over whether her love for Melanie is a sin, and her internal battle to accept her sexuality. It also suggests that in 'blowing her own trumpet', in being confident about the value of her relationship with Melanie, that she has indeed caused the metaphorical walls that offer security to fall. In this revision, Jeanette is the Joshua figure, asserting her belief that she is acting according to God's wishes and that her actions are good and right. This is significant because, although Jeanette is forced to leave her particular church, she has no desire to give up her religious beliefs. The possibility of crossing back into the garden also seems to express this exile from her church, but not from her Christian belief in God.

Joshua successor to Moses, who led the Israelites to the Promised Land. The Book of Joshua traces the history of the Israelites and their gradual conquest of Canaan (modern-day Palestine), and its division among the twelve tribes of Israel

the words of St Paul 'Unto the pure all things are pure; but unto them that are defiled and unbelieving is nothing pure; but even their mind and conscience is defiled' (St Paul's epistle to Titus, 1:15)

Beowulf probably the earliest epic poem in Old English, thought to have been written in the eighth century; combining Norse legend with Christian values, it describes the hero Beowulf's defeat of the monster Grendel

Humours obsolete medical term for the four fluids of the body (blood, phlegm, choler, melancholy), which are said to determine temperament

White Queen character in *Through the Looking Glass and What Alice Found There* by Lewis Carroll (1832–98)

Who will cast the first stone? in his defence of an adulterous woman, Jesus said, 'He that is without sin among you, let him first cast a stone at her' (John 8: 3–8); a warning against self-righteousness and a reminder that all men are sinners

Is she waving?...Drowning reference to a poem by Stevie Smith (1902–71): 'I was much too far out all my life / And not waving but drowning'

Euphrates in the Bible, the river that bounded the land promised to Joshua and the Chosen People (Joshua 1:4)

Garden...tree in the biblical myth of the Garden of Eden, Adam and Eve were forbidden by God to eat the fruit from the Tree of Knowledge; Satan tempted Eve, who ate the fruit and tempted Adam to eat it also; they were cast out of the garden as a consequence; the Tree of Life is believed to confer immortality; the Tree of Knowledge is found in the midst of the garden and is said to confer wisdom, which implies sexual knowledge (Genesis 2:9)

JUDGES   Jeanette and Katy's relationship is discovered; Jeanette leaves home and the church

Jeanette's mother forces Jeanette to leave home after she and Katy are discovered in bed together at the Morecambe guest house for the bereaved. In her explanation of the situation to the malicious friend of her mother who has discovered them, Jeanette protects Katy but incriminates herself. Her mother's response is to smash 'every plate in the kitchenette' (p. 128) and to voice her bitter reproach. When the pastor arrives, he and her mother disagree about whether Jeanette is the victim of a demon or is wilfully choosing to sin. Jeanette's presence at the Sisterhood meeting the following day **ironically** causes mayhem since the 'sisters' do not know how to respond to her. Only Elsie is kind, offering Jeanette tea, acceptance and friendship; she is only angry that she could not have done more to protect her from the actions of the other members of the church. She informs Jeanette that Miss Jewsbury is living, presumably with a female partner, in Leeds.

The pastor consults the church council about Jeanette's lesbianism, and the council's explanation for her sin echoes her mother's simplistic and stereotypically homophobic understanding of Jeanette's sexuality. The council also decides that her lesbianism is caused by 'aping men', namely taking a prominent role as a preacher, which should be reserved for men. To Jeanette's great shock, her mother, one of the most powerful women in the church, duplicitously states her agreement that women's roles in the church should be limited. This in effect concurs with the notion that women's faith and spirituality is inferior to that of men, who in the **patriarchal** institution of the Christian Church are traditionally held to be the real representatives of God on Earth. Elsie speaks out against this but collapses with the effort. As others help her home, the pastor issues an ultimatum to Jeanette, setting out what she must do in order to remain within the church. When the pastor calls the following day, Jeanette informs him and her mother that she is leaving the church and refuses the concessions they make to try to dissuade her. In order to be able to act on her decision, Jeanette must repress the immense pain and confusion she feels about her mother's betrayal and duplicity (at a personal and spiritual level). She goes to live with one of her teachers, but must take on another weekend job in order to support herself.

> As Jeanette's lesbianism is once more publicly exposed and denounced as perversity and a sin, we see how far she has progressed in her acceptance of her sexuality and of the consequences of leaving her family and the church. The fears expressed in the earlier fantasy sections and dreams are realised when Jeanette's inability to tolerate the restrictions placed on her sexuality and on her expression of her faith force her beyond the walls of the church and her family. Jeanette's refusal to deny her sexuality and to accept the patriarchal dictates of the church, which would strip her of her central role, govern her choice to leave the church and home. At the crisis point of her mother and the pastor debating her culpability, she again hallucinates about animated oranges. However, she realises that acknowledging and defending

her sexuality at a **metaphorical** or **symbolic** level is no longer sufficient; 'I was going to need more than an icon to get me through this one' (p. 130). In the face of her mother's rage and fierce homophobia, Jeanette's explanation of her sexuality is calm and reasoned, and her logical response to her mother's intolerance effectively undermines negative and reductive views of her sexuality.

However, Jeanette's deep-seated emotional trauma now becomes more clearly focused on coping with her mother's betrayal and with the fact that her bond with her mother is hard to break. Jeanette's confused and contradictory feelings for her mother are explored **allegorically** in the Sir Perceval narratives. These make reference to the legend of King Arthur and the Round Table and also echo earlier fantasy sections. They express Jeanette's unspoken feelings of love and loyalty that she has for her mother, yet also indirectly articulate her bitter anger and sense of loss at her mother's betrayal. They develop the theme of exile from her mother and her church family, and the pain that this entails. These sections also convey her sense of the collapse of the world she knew and trusted in, her need to discover herself, and a recognition of the emotional and physical hardship this brings. They also hint at what Jeanette may hope would be her mother's sense of loss; King Arthur (representative of her mother) longs for Sir Perceval, 'the darling, the favourite' (implicitly Jeanette) to return (p. 133).

Judges seventh book of the Old Testament; traces the history of the Israelites from Joshua's death to the time of Samuel; describes the exploits of various leaders (judges) from the time of entry into Canaan

Determinism a philosophy that all actions and events are determined by causes outside our will

Now I give you fair warning…off from *Alice's Adventures in Wonderland* by Lewis Carroll (1832–98); the Queen's full speech continues: '…and that in about half no time! Take your choice!' Her petulance is used to mock Jeanette's mother's rash anger; this, plus the threat of decapitation, also recalls the similar behaviour of the Prince, who sought the perfect woman

Havelock Ellis and inversion Ellis (1859–1939) pioneered the science of sexology, putting forward explanations of homosexuality and theorising its causes and range of expression; his theory of inversion suggests that

homosexuality is caused by a mismatch of body and soul; female inversion
is the result of a male soul being trapped in a female body. Although this
theory is now outdated, its significance for Jeanette's argument with her
mother lies in the fact that it posits homosexuality as something congenital
rather than a choice

Sir Perceval a hero of Arthurian legend and the keeper of the Holy Grail
(see p. 27)

Arthur a Celtic chieftain of sixth-century Wales; stories of his court are
infused into the legends of King Arthur told in medieval romances

Camelot location of King Arthur's court, believed by some to be Winchester

Holy Grail see p. 27

Sir Gawain nephew of King Arthur and one of the most outstanding of the
Round Table knights; renowned for his purity and courage

The Round Table a circular table designed to seat King Arthur and his one
hundred and fifty knights so that all would be of equal importance

Launcelot and Bors Launcelot is the most famous of the knights of the
Round Table; lover of Queen Guinevere, he was exiled by King Arthur but
returned when Arthur was dead; Bors, uncle of Launcelot, was another
knight of the Round Table

stone that held a bright sword King Arthur's sword, Excalibur, was magically
fixed in a stone and could be drawn out only by the rightful king of England

Hebrews book of the New Testament

painted the white roses red possibly refers to the War of the Roses, a thirty-
year struggle for the Crown between the House of York (symbolised by a
white rose) and the House of Lancaster (a red rose)

R UTH   **Jeanette works at a funeral parlour and also sells ice-cream.
Elsie dies. Jeanette goes to work at a psychiatric hospital
before going away; one Christmas holiday she returns
home**

Jeanette has two jobs in order to support herself financially – laying out
bodies at the Elysium Fields Funeral Parlour and selling ice-cream.
Although Joe and the woman who own the undertaker's are kind,
Jeanette finds it hard to join in their conversations and cannot really
communicate with them. She recalls happy memories of buying ice-
cream as a child. Such happiness is contrasted with the news of Elsie's

death. A crowd outside Elsie's house attracts Jeanette's attention. Inside her mother bluntly tells her 'Elsie's dead' (p. 146) and the pastor, trying to make Jeanette regret her actions, succeeds in causing her even more anguish. Jeanette gets more information about Elsie's death from the queue of women waiting to buy ice-creams. Mrs White comes to reprimand Jeanette for 'Making money out of the dead'; she cries and Jeanette offers some sympathy, but Mrs White refuses to tell her when the funeral will be. Jeanette is so distraught that she takes two days off work.

Joe informs Jeanette that Elsie is at Elysium Fields; after writing a letter, she goes to the funeral parlour. She does not look in on Elsie until the woman and Joe have gone to the cinema and she has thoroughly cleaned the hearse for Elsie's funeral. Sitting most of the night with Elsie, Jeanette tells her about her feelings and her hopes for the future. Unexpectedly, Jeanette has to serve the food at Elsie's funeral meal the following day. All goes well until the vicar arrives and detains Joe, which means that Jeanette must face her mother, the pastor and the others when she serves the ice-cream. Affronted, they leave, and Jeanette's mother disowns Jeanette. Joe dismisses them as 'mad', but seeing them makes Jeanette realise how isolated she feels. Miss Jewsbury arrives and Jeanette tells her of her plans; Miss Jewsbury offers to help Jeanette if she needs it. Shortly after this, Jeanette gets a live-in job at a psychiatric hospital.

There is a gap in the realist narrative about Jeanette's final departure for the city, and this event is only indirectly related via the Winnet and Sir Perceval stories. The Winnet story, which begins this chapter and weaves through the first half of it, retells the events of Jeanette's life as a modern fairy tale. There are obvious parallels between Jeanette's and Winnet's experience (as indeed between their names). Winnet's practical, emotional and psychological preparations to leave for the beautiful city can be read as an **allegory** for Jeanette's similar departure. Winnet's acceptance that this is an irrevocable move, and the trepidation and determination with which she sets sail we assume are also Jeanette's feelings. In the city Jeanette reflects on her attachment to home and to the past, yet also on the danger of returning because this would mean the denial of her newly discovered self and life. She finds it impossible to discuss her mother, and reflects that had she remained at home, she would only have been able to follow a pre-written path in life. Instead, she has chosen the troubled uncertainty of being a 'prophet'.

Twice we are told that she 'came to this city to escape', and in a **metaphorical** way, resonant with echoes of earlier fantasy sections, she describes her feeling of being protected by the city walls and of achieving her ambitions, although this is necessarily a lonely experience. Despite the desire to escape the past and her attachments, however, she feels compelled to return home. She goes during the Christmas holidays, and as she gets closer to home, her feelings of danger, fear and longing are expressed in terms of the real becoming increasingly unreal and of feeling, like Winnet and Sir Perceval, inexplicably drawn into a magical sphere of enchantment.

Jeanette arrives home and it is as if she has never been away. Her mother is playing carols on her new electronic organ and gives Jeanette an extensive demonstration of it. She tells Jeanette of two church scandals – the embezzlement of church funds by the society's secretary to pay off gambling debts and wife maintenance, and the threatened closure of the Morecambe guest house because of poor hygiene. To add to her mother's horror, the guest house had also started holding seances. They briefly discuss what Jeanette is doing. On an errand to the shops, Jeanette calls in to see Mrs Arkwright, who takes her to the Cock and Whistle. She complains about the decline in her pest-control business because of improvements in housing, and confides her plan of committing arson and setting up a tourist business in Torremolinos with the insurance money.

As she continues on her errand, Jeanette feels confused by the mixed responses to her return – Mrs Arkwright took a few minutes to remember her, Betty at Trickett's café has forgotten her, and her mother seems not to have noticed her absence. She ponders on the idea of parallel existence: 'I am still an evangelist in the North, as well as the person who ran away' (p. 164). Climbing the hill, she reflects on her immeasurable longing for love, passion and devotion of biblical proportions, and on her keenly felt need never to be betrayed again. As she gazes over the town, she spots Melanie's house and remembers their most recent encounter; again Jeanette has a bitter sense of betrayal when Melanie dismisses their relationship as insignificant and suggests that Jeanette destroy any evidence of it. As at other moments, Jeanette's anger is expressed in a patronising attitude and cutting sarcasm towards the person causing her pain. Although she feels that she is coming to terms with repressed emotions, she also feels as if she has not moved on, but come only full circle.

On Christmas Eve, Jeanette's mother's childish impatience and delight in her presents is a surprise to Jeanette. Again, her hypocrisy is mocked; her blessing is perfunctory in her rush to open her presents. One final shocking scandal connected with the Morecambe guest house for the bereaved sends her mother into a rage. Although she knows that her family is far from perfect, an idea twice summed up with the image of chairs around a table and 'the right number of cups' (pp. 131, 171), Jeanette cannot completely detach herself from it. Her mother returns in a rage from telephoning Pastor Finch about the latest scandal, but in time for her broadcast. The chapter ends on an **ironic** note.

The Winnet and Sir Perceval sections again express feelings that Jeanette cannot, and convey her emotional and psychological states. With their focus on issues of family, belonging, disruption, betrayal, exile, quest, estrangement, mourning for the past and the desire to return, these sections echo and develop the significant aspects of Jeanette's experience, and explore and bring together these key themes of the novel. For example, Winnet's experience of never being fully fluent in the new language she has to learn outside the sorcerer's kingdom expresses Jeanette's more vague and abstract sense of alienation in the world outside the church. Although Jeanette speaks the same language as the woman and Joe at the funeral parlour, she too feels 'foreign' and isolated, since she does not share their views on the world and feels unable to communicate fully with them. Similarly, Sir Perceval's unease in his unprotected, limbo-like state in the woods can be seen to express the practical and emotional difficulty experienced during the transitional stage before Jeanette could act decisively to break free; for Sir Perceval, and implicitly for Jeanette, feelings of uncertainty and a longing for home and what is familiar, counteract the desire to fulfil his quest. Both stories also stress the need for self-exploration and self-knowledge before the unknown world beyond what is familiar can be faced without fear.

There is an increasing blurring between the realist and fantasy sections as they move closer together, with elements from previous fairy tales and dreams recurring, and as the Winnet, Perceval and Jeanette stories share similar elements. These include the rough brown pebble, the raven who has lost chances for happiness and, importantly, the thread that connects the parent and child figures. The recurrence of this thread in all three narrative strands suggests how powerful and compelling the pull of home is for Jeanette. However, her allegorical counterpart, Sir Perceval, also suggests an alternative to what seems an inevitable return and entrapment in the familiarity of her old life. At the point at which both he and Jeanette feel their quest is futile and the lure of home is strong, Sir Perceval dreams that he is a spider dangling on a thread and that a raven (a friend in the Winnet story) cuts through this thread to liberate him. This alternative course is a possibility that Jeanette chooses not to act on; it may be that such an action is impossible to countenance (suggested by its doubly embedded expression in a dream within an allegorical section). It could also be that some awareness of the possibility of cutting her ties enables Jeanette to retain a sense of control over her choice to maintain contact with her mother, regardless of the danger of being drawn in by her mother's influence.

The Winnet and Sir Perceval stories seem to reframe Jeanette's experience as a more traditional clash between parent and child over the child's increasing maturity and choices, which disrupt the parent's plans and expectations. The Winnet story shifts the emphasis away from Jeanette's sexuality as the problem and the cause of strife between parent and child. In this fairy tale, it is the sorcerer's inability to adapt his expectations, to accept his daughter's desires and choices, and his petulant refusal to allow her to diverge in any way from his plan for her future that lead to her exile from the kingdom. Winnet's apprenticeship to her father can in part be read as the sequel to the fairy tale of apprenticeship, which explained Jeanette's mother's decision to enter the church in the first chapter. If we read the princess of the first tale in Genesis and the sorcerer of the Winnet fairy tale as counterparts for Jeanette's mother, and Winnet as a fairy-tale counterpart for Jeanette, we can

see that it is her mother's inability to accept that Jeanette will not
bend to her will and become a missionary that is the cause of the rift
between them. The Sir Perceval story also shifts the emphasis away
from the child as the cause of the parent-child rift; his quest is a
worthy one – to seek the Holy Grail and to find peace and harmony
– but it is King Arthur's sorrowful response to this that causes
distress. Both suggest that the split between Jeanette and her
mother is common to all families, and is a consequence of the child
becoming an adult.

By the end of the novel, Jeanette's mother does seem to have
changed in some respects. The shocks of the Morecambe guest
house and the Society for the Lost seem to have humbled her, and
she is trying to move with the times, broadening her influence
beyond the immediate community in which she lives with her CB
radio. Her eagerness to show Jeanette the capabilities of her
electronic organ, her childish rush to open her presents, and her
sadistic glee at getting a catapult are reminiscent of Jeanette as a
child. This suggests that Jeanette's perception of her mother has
changed; her passionate conviction and commitment to her faith
are longer experienced by Jeanette as dangerously overwhelming.

However, her mother is still the centre of her world and
things are made to revolve around her. She remains domineering
and obsessive; she is still at war with the demon, especially
homosexuality, as her self-help kit suggests. In a reversal of the
way she planned to use Jeanette to further her status in the church,
she now uses Jeanette's 'sin' as a basis for forging a new role for
herself, joining Pastor Finch in his 'demon bus' and helping the
parents of other 'demon-possessed children' (p. 169). It would seem
that her mother has also modified her narrow-minded dogmatism
by acknowledging that 'oranges are not the only fruit'; however, this
can also be seen as misleading. This change in opinion only
expresses her continuing inability to understand difference, racial or
in terms of sexuality. Her CB radio name, Kindly Light, seems to
offer hope that she *has* become more kindly, and that she, taking
the name of one of Elsie's favourite hymns, may now be able
to express the maternal love and acceptance towards Jeanette

that Elsie did. However, this name forms the final irony of the novel, as her mother storms into the house in a rage and slams the door, immediately signing on to her CB broadcast as Kindly Light.

Ruth eighth book of the Old Testament; tells of a Moabite woman, Ruth, who is devoted to her mother-in-law, Naomi; after the death of her husband, Ruth remarries and has a son, whom Naomi treats as her own

Shadrach, Meshach and Abednego see p. 21

Elysium Fields in Greek mythology the fields at the ends of the earth, where chosen heroes became gods; has come to mean a place or state of ideal happiness

Pinny abbreviation of 'pinafore'

Great Exhibition first international exhibition of the products of industry, held in Crystal Palace, London, in 1851

Gary Cooper Hollywood actor (1901–61); played diffident heroes, as in his most famous film *High Noon* (1952)

When did you last see your mother? in Malory's tale of the quest for the Holy Grail, Sir Perceval's aunt asks him a similar question: 'Whan herde you tydynges if youre modir?' and goes on to tell him that she died of sorrow soon after Sir Perceval departed for his new life with the knights of the Round Table

Lot's wife she and her husband were inhabitants of the iniquitous city of Sodom; they escaped its destruction by fire and brimstone, but Lot's wife disobeyed God's orders and looked back at the burning city; she was turned into a pillar of salt as a punishment

Middlemarch novel by George Eliot (Mary Ann Evans, 1819–80), who abandoned evangelical Christianity and led a free-thinking life that put her at odds with many people; her writings often reflect the constrained life of women in Victorian times

pompadour a hairstyle raised high above the forehead; Jeanette's mother uses this word by mistake – she means 'paramour', an illicit lover

a great cracking...samite paraphrase of Malory's *Morte d'Arthur*, when the Holy Grail (see p. 27) appears; the incident that triggers the quest and causes the break-up of the Round Table (see p. 43)

PART THREE

CRITICAL APPROACHES

CHARACTERISATION

Winterson creates her characters largely through their speech and actions; what they say and how they say it reveals their personality, class, beliefs, and their view of the world and themselves. There is little comment on their physical appearance, but we do get a strong sense of them through the tone used to describe their behaviour and their interactions with others. Many of the characters are treated with humour, which ranges from gentle mockery to create a sense of an endearing character (such as Elsie), to more scathing ridicule, which generates hostile feelings towards that character (such as Pastor Finch).

As might be expected, references to biblical figures help to create a sense of character, though the tone with which such **allusions** are made is important to the sense we get of the character. For instance, Jeanette aligns herself unquestioningly with 'good' male figures in the Bible to convey the sense that she is good and can have a legitimate place in the church; her mother's identification with the Virgin Mary, on the other hand, leads to our finding her arrogant and sets her up for ridicule. Exposing the ways in which the various characters use the church and religion to express their desire for power is also used to convey a sense of character.

The female characters are central to this novel, while the male characters are marginalised and treated largely with mockery. For the most part, the characters are static and do not develop, with the obvious exceptions of Jeanette and, to a lesser extent, her mother and Miss Jewsbury.

JEANETTE

Jeanette develops throughout the novel and although her experience alters the way she sees the world, she continues to be self-assured and confident, outspoken and strong – qualities she has learned from her mother. Her isolated childhood and unusual upbringing set her apart from other children, but the conviction that she is right (also learned from her mother) means that she survives not only the ostracism of school, but also, later, the church's attack on her sexuality. She refuses to accept either the church's interpretation of her desire as a 'sin' or Miss Jewsbury's conceptualisation of lesbian sexuality as a 'problem'. For Jeanette her sexuality is yet another sign that she is 'special', and she insists that her sexuality is only a problem because of the homophobia of others. In places, this assertion of being right borders on arrogance and intolerance. For instance, Jeanette's own religious intolerance is apparent in her discussion with Melanie about her plans to study theology at university. The narrative technique employed, however, aims to keep the reader on Jeanette's side, and here, the fact that her destiny as a missionary is in doubt because she gets sunstroke (even in Paignton), humorously dispels any hostile response we might have to her own dogmatic views (p. 101).

She learns much from her mother and from her mother's role in the church. Jeanette learns to be strong and outspoken, important qualities when she comes to defend her sexuality. Although she breaks from her mother's faith and outlook on life, her mother's subversive strategies of interpretation, her practice of revisionary storytelling and her fierce commitment clearly influence her whole life. 'She inherits her mother's strength of conviction, her principled insistence on pursuing openly what she thinks is right, her passion, her logic and her combativeness' (Marshment and Hallam in *The Good, the Bad and the Gorgeous*, eds Hamer and Budge, p. 157). She also repeatedly identifies herself with male figures of the Bible (Jesus, Joshua and Daniel) and in doing so writes herself into a patriarchal tradition and aligns herself with the good and righteous in answer to those who would categorise her as demon-possessed.

Jeanette's **allegorical** and fairy-tale counterparts also contribute to our sense of her as a character. Winterson seems to be suggesting that identity is complex and contradictory. These counterparts work through painful experiences, express unspeakable emotions, and also suggest the possibility of making different choices. This kind of characterisation opens up our sense of Jeanette as a character. It frees our understanding of her from the rigid and restrictive historically specific notions of gender and class, which play a large part in determining her identity in the realist narrative. In the fantasy sections, gender boundaries are frequently blurred, with male characters exhibiting stereotypically feminine behaviour and vice versa. As critic Tess Cosslett argues, 'a kind of composite character emerges in the last chapter: Jeanette/ Winnet/ Ruth/ Perceval/Jane, all united in exile and questing' (*Postmodern Studies 25*, eds Grice and Woods, p. 24).

JEANETTE'S MOTHER (LOUIE)

A powerful woman both in her own home and in the church, Jeanette's mother is domineering and forcibly asserts her views. As critic Susan Rubin Suleiman states, 'Repressive and fanatical, she looms large' (in *Avant Garde 4*, 1990, p. 137). Two other critics, Margaret Marshment and Julia Hallam, compare her to 'popular images of Margaret Thatcher as prime minister. As dogmatic and powerful middle-aged women, they both invite the same mix of admiration, incredulity, disapproval and passionate hatred' (in *The Good, the Bad and the Gorgeous*, eds Hamer and Budge, p. 157). Implicit parallels with Napoleon also highlight her pride, vanity and her megalomaniacal pursuit of her ambitions, as well as suggesting her charismatic charm.

She is selfish, ruthless, determined, forceful, provocative, petulant and hubristic, and sulks if God does not concur with her will for destruction. From the outset, her absolutist world view is the target for mockery, and her pride, vanity and belligerent narrow-mindedness are all treated with irony. In particular, religion seems to be an outlet for her intolerance, hatred and resentment, and expresses her refusal to compromise, her inability to see both sides of an issue or to have mixed feelings. The church is also an arena in which she can enact her quest for power and influence and in which she can assert her views with authority and follow her ambitions. For her, religion is not a self-sacrificing, disinterested, genuinely felt belief; indeed, her conversion story belies the fact that her faith has ulterior motives. Jeanette is very much a pawn in her mother's 'tag match' game and is compelled to fulfil her mother's sense of competition by winning the Bible quizzes.

Her refusal to allow her maternal role to hinder her career in the church, and her disparagement of men in general – 'We had no Wise Men because she didn't believe there were any wise men' (p. 3) – and

Jeanette's father in particular seem to be tapping into typical **feminist** ideas. However, despite her own power at a localised level in the church, she is a staunch defender of the patriarchal hierarchy and the values of the institution. She is repeatedly shown to be in thrall to the male figures of authority, blushing at Pastor Finch's compliment about her sandwiches and idolising Pastor Spratt. She readily accepts a restriction of her influence and role after Jeanette's lesbianism is perceived as a threat by the men in the church.

Her extremism and sense of superiority ostracise her from most people. Only May and Mrs White seem to be her friends; others consider her to be 'mad'. Her class snobbery also highlights a lack of fairness in her judgement; we are told directly 'she never was particularly fair' when Jeanette reveals her mother's prejudice against those who shopped at Maxi Ball's. There are also several instances where she is mockingly shown to be hypocritical, and for the most part it is her desires and appetite for what is forbidden that cause her to compromise her principles. For example, her taste for black peas leads her to buy from the gypsies, whom she defines as 'fornicators' (and therefore enemies), and she also goes to great lengths to validate her appetite for 'unclean' shrimps. It could be argued that this compulsion to satisfy her appetites and her reinterpretation of biblical doctrine in order to make space for her own desires is something else that Jeanette inherits, the desire in Jeanette's case being sexual.

Her role in the church exempts her (in her own eyes at least) from many of the traditional duties of motherhood. She is often 'with the Lord' when convention dictates that she should be caring for her child. Repeatedly she offers oranges as a substitute for her presence – an acidic replacement for maternal love and affection. This contrasts with the fleshy 'plums of indignation' **metaphorically** falling from the mothers who go to the school to complain about Jeanette's behaviour in order to protect and defend their children.

By the end of the novel she seems to change a little, although this is debatable. The shocks of the church scandals seem to have humbled her, though not shaken her faith. Her new awareness that 'oranges are not the only fruit' also seems to suggest a change to her single-minded and dogmatic view of the world. However, this is somewhat misleading. Her notion that pineapple is an appropriate food for a black pastor only

confirms her limited recognition of alternatives to her own experience
and her inability to empathise with those she considers different from
herself. Her CB call is Kindly Light (the name of one of Elsie's favourite
hymns), and this seems to offer hope that she has become more like
Elsie – kindly and able to express love and acceptance to Jeanette.
However, the world is still made to revolve around her, and she remains
domineering, obsessive and still at war with the demon, especially
homosexuality, as her self-help kit suggests.

ELSIE NORRIS

'Testifying Elsie' is occasionally set up for gentle mockery because of her
eccentricity and eagerness to see God's actions in even the most
mundane, everyday experiences. Her absent-mindedness is also treated
with comic humour. However, she is a balanced and dignified figure, and
with her pragmatic approach to religion, plus her interests in art,
literature and music, she acts as an alternative role model for Jeanette. She
is a mother figure for Jeanette, as well as being her friend, and provides
maternal love, support and comfort. She consistently acts in Jeanette's
interests and takes her side, offering her the care, protection and comfort
her mother does not. She plays a major role in Jeanette's formative years
and provides a sense of balance against her mother's fanatical behaviour
and way of seeing the world. Later, she plays a crucial role in shielding
Jeanette and Melanie from the wrath of the church and offers them a
haven in which their relationship can grow.

Elsie's friendship offers Jeanette access to ideas that contradict her
mother's restricted and restrictive views. She introduces her to a range of
Western cultural texts, opening her mind to expressions of feeling and
visions of reality other than the one her mother offers. Elsie teaches her
the importance of stories, and although the adult perspective and
interests she develops further isolate her from the children at school, the
tenets of Elsie's philosophy help her to survive in the secular world.
Jeanette learns the importance of 'balance and vision', the validity of
plural interpretations, the value of imagination and perseverance, the joy
of rebuilding and renewal, and power of the mind to determine the future
(see Exodus). In the face of Jeanette's mother's disapproval, Elsie also
conspires with Jeanette over her choice of non-religious themes for her

models in an attempt to support Jeanette in her desire for success and recognition. Her prominence in Exodus also suggests that she is a Moses figure, leading the Israelite Jeanette to the Promised Land of imagination and a more balanced, informed and tolerant view of the world.

MISS JEWSBURY

Pronounced 'not holy' by Mrs White (p. 25), Miss Jewsbury is the only church member (apart from Elsie) who acts in Jeanette's interests when the church's extremism threatens to harm her. She forcefully steps in to ensure that Jeanette gets medical attention for her deafness when she is a child, takes her home after the public denunciation of her 'sin', and later returns for Elsie's funeral, offering Jeanette support. She reveals Elsie's role in protecting Jeanette and Melanie, a role entrusted to her when Elsie had to go into hospital. She also acts as a foil for Jeanette's integrity, honesty and open defence of her sexuality. Jeanette rejects Miss Jewsbury's definition of lesbianism as a 'problem', and their love-making, in the wake of what for Jeanette was a profoundly shocking experience of being accused of sin, is somewhat disturbing. However, Elsie's pointed revelation that Miss Jewsbury is living with someone in Leeds suggests that Miss Jewsbury does change and comes to accept her lesbian sexuality.

MELANIE

Like Jeanette, Melanie is from a working-class home; her father is dead and she lives with her mother. Although she is committed to her newly found faith, she wants to study theology at university so that she can have an informed understanding of beliefs. While the relationship with Melanie is profoundly important to Jeanette, the significance for Melanie is more ambiguous. She later gets married and has children, and in the final conversation Jeanette recalls having with her she seems to be dismissing their past as insignificant. However, these recollections are entirely subjective and coloured by Jeanette's complex feelings of anger, betrayal and sense of loss, and Melanie's actions are far from unambiguous. During her Christmas visit in the first year after she has left for university she tries hard to see Jeanette; she carries mistletoe and offers her an orange. Even their final encounter, where Melanie suggests that Jeanette destroy any evidence of their relationship, is ambiguous – if, as she says, this part of her past means nothing, her concern to eliminate all trace of it could suggest otherwise. Jeanette's relationship with Melanie is, of course, a crucial factor in Jeanette's break with her mother. Humorously, at a metaphorical level her name (given because as a baby she 'looked like a melon', p. 81) represents a challenge to Jeanette's mother's narrow-minded dogmatism, expressed in the phrase 'oranges are the only fruit'.

KATY

Like Melanie, Katy is also from a working-class background and similarly joins Jeanette's church. Jeanette and Katy's relationship is far less intense and fraught than that of Jeanette and Melanie; it is stable and long term, seeming to be based on friendship as much as sexual attraction. Their relationship is significant not only because it gives Jeanette the confidence to come out to her mother and the church again, but because it also enables her to defend her sexuality in the face of inevitable hostility and rejection. Unlike Melanie, Katy is kind and sensitive, notably to Jeanette's trauma caused by Melanie's Christmas visit. However, she is not as fully rounded a character as Melanie. In many ways she is more of a 'functional' character, her function apparently being to help Jeanette fully accept her sexuality and to act as a catalyst for Jeanette's assertion of her lesbianism. This interpretation of her role is confirmed by Katy's disappearance from the novel after Jeanette has left home.

THE PASTORS

Both Pastor Finch and Pastor Spratt are treated with derision, their authority and views comically undercut and their devoted expression of faith treated with ridicule. Although within the church they have great power, they are named after a small bird and a small fish, which suggests that outside such a rigidly **patriarchal** institution their real importance would be minimal.

Roy Finch, from Stockport, is married to Grace, whose concern that he does not overtax himself in his religious fervour undercuts the power of his fanaticism (pp. 12, 82). He is boastful of 'the mighty gift' God has given him in his talent for purging sinners of their demon; his sermons are comically **melodramatic**, and his excessive bongo accompaniment to his newly composed hymn is presented as ridiculous. As a child, Jeanette reflects on how 'horrible' he is: he is physically unappealing and his attempt to speak with an authoritative 'manly' voice is mocked. 'His teeth stuck out, and his voice was squeaky, even though he tried to make it deep and stern. Poor Mrs Finch. How did she live with him?' (p. 13).

Pastor Spratt, on the other hand, is the charismatic opportunist who uses carefully devised marketing strategies to persuade people to the faith. Largely seen through Jeanette's mother's adoring eyes, he is depicted as an 'action-hero' missionary whose 'conquests' and successes abroad win him great accolades within the church.

JEANETTE'S FATHER (JACK)

A direct contrast to his wife, Jeanette's father is a 'Joseph' figure to her mother's central role as the 'Virgin Mary'. He is presented as passive and easy-going, although getting no proper Sunday dinner 'depressed him', and he does occasionally subtly rebel against his wife's authority – watching the wrestling on television on a Sunday, for instance. As a child, Jeanette has a bond with him, and they are united in the face of her mother's assertion that what she thinks is right. They are allies and escape her overbearing presence by spending time in the outside toilet. Jeanette expresses sympathy for her father, 'Poor dad', a counter to her mother's sometimes fond expression of dissatisfaction with him, he 'was never quite good enough' and did not 'push himself' enough (pp. 11, 8). The rift with her family because of her marriage to a working-class gambler may in part explain her mother's attitude, but this also suggests that her feelings for him were strong. He is absent from the majority of the novel, but his successful choice of Christmas gift for her mother suggests a compatibility between them.

MRS WHITE AND MAY

These are two contrasting members of the church. Mrs White's obsession with holiness is consistently presented as ridiculous; her phrase 'it's not holy' signals that she is quick to judge, and absolute in her categorisation of what is good. Her fanaticism is often ridiculed, one example being the Sunday when she was intent on finding out whether Next Door were 'fornicating'. The language used has a comic effect, suggesting her desperate curiosity and also her struggle to have her self-righteous sense of outrage confirmed: she 'immediately crushed her ear against the wall', strained to hear by 'clamping herself back against the wall', and 'slithered up and down the skirting board' to find a good place for the glass (p. 52). Although she is as extreme as Jeanette's mother in terms of her religious belief, unlike Louie, she is a nervous and ineffectual woman, though more rigorously principled (she will not go to the Rechabite hall, for instance). The name White seems entirely apt for this woman, whose principles are based on an absolute sense of holiness.

May's attitude to her faith is far more balanced. She has interests outside the church, such as bingo. She also has women friends, such as Mrs Arkwright and Ida from the newsagent's, whom Jeanette's mother and Mrs White frown upon.

MRS ARKWRIGHT, THE WOMAN AND JOE

These figures create a sense of the environment outside the church in which Jeanette grows up. Mrs Arkwright has her own vermin-eradication business and her constant complaint is that it is not doing well. She has grand plans to capitalise on the tourist trade in the rapidly developing Spanish holiday resort of Torremolinos. She is always kind to Jeanette and her down-to-earth pronouncements about her mother and the church ring true for the girl. Again, this offers a counterbalance to the fanaticism of the church in which Jeanette is caught up.

The woman is never named, but she too struggles with her floristry business until she goes into partnership with an undertaker, Joe. They are kind to Jeanette and do their best to give her support when she leaves home. Joe is a considerate man and sensitive to the needs of the bereaved. He forms a contrast to the other men, inside and outside the church, such as Jeanette's Uncle Bill, and Frank and Bert, the husbands whom Doreen and Nellie complain bitterly about, who are negatively depicted as insensitive, violent, insulting, drunken and adulterous.

QUEST FOR IDENTITY

Both Jeanette and her mother are engaged in a quest to attain a sense of identity beyond the limitations placed on them as relatively poor women in a male-dominated, class-prejudiced society. Both are, in a sense, marginalised figures – Jeanette because of her sexuality and her mother because of her faith. Their difference from mainstream society causes them to be ostracised, but their sense of being 'called to be apart' (p. 42) simultaneously enables them to forge an identity for themselves in defiance of the culturally prescribed roles for women.

Both are, in a way, orphans: Jeanette's mother is abandoned by her middle-class family when she marries Jack, and Jeanette is given up for adoption. This seems to offer the opportunity for self-creation, as it does for the many orphaned characters in nineteenth-century fiction, among them Jane Eyre, whose life story resonates in many ways with the 'real' and imagined life stories of Jeanette and her mother. Jeanette's mother's revision of the plot of *Jane Eyre*, so that Jane marries the ambitious missionary St John Rivers rather than the passionate Byronic hero Rochester, is often read as her projection of the devoted life of a missionary she plans for Jeanette. However, her retelling of Charlotte Brontë's plot could also be read as her own imagined life as the wife of the ambitious missionary she adores, Pastor Spratt. For both women, stories of all kinds are crucial in constructing their identities. In part, Jeanette's mother uses the story of the Virgin Mary as a model, allowing her to create a central role for herself within the church. Describing herself as a 'missionary on the home front' also enables her to disregard conventional roles for women and to single-mindedly pursue her ambition for power.

Among the stories that Jeanette draws on in her quest for identity are biblical myths, fairy tales and Arthurian legends. Her many fantasy counterparts illustrate how complex and traumatic this quest can be, given the limitations placed on her because of her gender, sexuality and class. Jeanette identifies herself with unquestionably 'good' male figures in the Bible – Jesus, Daniel and Joshua – in an attempt to forge a positive place for herself within the patriarchal institution of the church. Sir Perceval is another male counterpart for Jeanette, although his ambiguous gender identity ('He was a warrior who longed to grow herbs',

p. 161) highlights further Jeanette's desire to escape the fixed and limited notions of gender that would compromise her quest for identity. In both the realist and fantasy narratives, Jeanette's quest entails a break from the manipulative control of her mother. Most obviously, the sorcerer's desire to know Winnet's name represents the power Jeanette feels her mother exerts; to name is to possess and control, and this fairy tale plays out the conflict between Jeanette and her mother for control over Jeanette's future and identity.

EXILE AND RETURN

This theme emerges in the Joshua chapter and becomes increasingly important in the closing chapters of the novel. In the realist narrative, Jeanette feels compelled to return to visit her mother, regardless of her mother's betrayal and the bizarre and far from ordinary family she recognises hers to be. It in no way resembles the romanticised ideal, summed up in the repeated image of a fireside scene with chairs around a table 'and the right number of cups' (pp. 131, 171). Reference to the pain of exile and the danger of return recurs in the fantasy sections in Joshua, in the numerous **allusions** to the biblical story of the Israelites leaving Egypt, and the mention of Lot's wife, who looked back and was turned into a pillar of salt (p. 155). This theme is also clearly played out in the Sir Perceval sections and, in particular, through parts of the biblical story of Ruth, alluded to in the final chapter.

In Sir Thomas Malory's retelling of the legendary tales of King Arthur and his knights of the Round Table, Sir Perceval and the other knights go in quest of the Holy Grail, leaving their king and their court. The fantasy sections in *Oranges* focus on Sir Perceval's intense feelings of homesickness, loss, loneliness and regret at leaving King Arthur, who is also pining and distressed to lose his favourite. Like Sir Perceval, Jeanette is compelled to leave home; her mother's betrayal and her own need to pursue her desires for love and education drive her on, despite her feelings of uncertainty and loneliness. For Sir Perceval, as for Jeanette, this exile from a parent figure is not his first such experience. He has left his mother in order to join the Round Table, with the sense that life must change; parting from his king and father-figure, however, causes him grief which is almost unbearable. Similarly, Jeanette's 'exile' from her biological mother caused her pain, but her complex feelings about her second exile are impossible to articulate: 'I know what I think, but words in the head are like voices under water. They are distorted' (p. 156). Despite her bitterness about her mother's betrayal, she, like Sir Perceval, longs to return home, drawn always by her love and sense of loyalty to her mother.

The Book of Ruth also foregrounds the themes of exile and return, bound up, as they are, with the idea of loyalty. In the biblical story, the focus is specifically on the strength and endurance of the mother–daughter bond and on loyalty between women in a **patriarchal** society, where only women's bonds with men are considered significant. Ruth is one of only two books in the Old Testament in which women have a central role, and it is concerned with Ruth's voluntary exile from her own family, religion and country in order to return to her mother-in-law, Naomi. Ruth's devotion to her mother-in-law parallels Jeanette's loyalty to her adoptive mother (a 'mother in law' in another sense). As critic Laurel Bollinger suggests, Winterson's use of the Book of Ruth points to 'a radical revaluing of connection between women' (in *Tulsa Studies in Women's Literature*, 13 (2), 1994, p. 369).

The fairy tale of Winnet also deals with the idea of exile, but simultaneously sets up the expectation of return when the sorcerer ties a piece of invisible thread around Winnet's button in order always to be able to draw her back. This idea of a thread linking child and parent figures recurs in the Sir Perceval sections and in the realist narrative, stressing the inevitability of return. Only in one of Sir Perceval's dreams is an alternative to return suggested when a raven (in the Winnet story, a friend advising her to leave her father) cuts through the spider's thread and liberates the spider/him. This expresses Jeanette's troubled ambivalence about her return to her mother and the reader may be surprised, angered or dismayed at even this temporary return, given the struggle she has had to break away to pursue her desires and ambitions.

SEXUALITY

The issue of sexuality is obviously a central one in the novel. Jeanette's lesbian sexuality becomes the focus of her traumatic break with her mother, and also seems to incite the most shocking acts of betrayal on her mother's part. What lies at the heart of this conflict is the polarised way sexuality is conceptualised, with heterosexuality and lesbian and gay sexualities being perceived as clearly demarcated, entirely separate and oppositional. However, close examination of the expressions and repressions of lesbian sexuality in the novel suggests that this simple duality is not so cut and dried.

Although Jeanette is eventually secure in her sexuality after a period of apparent denial, self-deception or deliberate pretence, the novel also suggests that sexual orientation and the models for sexual expression are culturally constructed. While sexuality may be experienced as something natural, like other cultural models for identity, such as gender, the constructions of sexuality can be questioned and undermined. This process of challenging culturally endorsed ideas about sexuality is suggested by the representation of sexuality as something that is fluid and not a limited choice of either/or. Sexuality **symbolised** through fruit is part of a long literary and cultural tradition. In this novel, the biblical symbol of forbidden sexual knowledge is revised so that the orange tree replaces the apple tree at the heart of the Edenic garden. However, the easy choice this revision seems to suggest – apples for heterosexuality, oranges for lesbian sexuality – is undermined by the fluidity of the orange symbolism itself. Oranges are used to represent a disparate number of things in this novel, such as Jeanette's mother's dogmatism, her lack of maternal care and Jeanette's lesbian integrity. As we are also repeatedly made aware, they are not the only fruit. This suggests the idea that there is a spectrum of sexual responses, and that individuals can locate their own sexual orientation along this spectrum differently at different times of their lives.

In the novel there are various expressions of lesbian sexuality: the women in the paper shop, though ostracised by some, live as an ordinary couple in the community. Miss Jewsbury, on the other hand, considers her sexuality to be a problem and seems to repress her lesbian desires until she moves to Leeds. Jeanette's mother's sexuality is also represented as complex. Although she is ostensibly heterosexual, she seems to shun physical intimacy with her husband – they sleep, unnecessarily, in shifts, and her 'attitude to the begetting of children' is a 'mysterious' one, 'it wasn't that she couldn't do it, more that she didn't want to do it' (p. 3). The photograph of a woman in the Old Flames section of her photograph album seems to cause her some uneasiness when Jeanette notices it, and Miss Jewsbury's comment that Jeanette's mother 'knows about feelings, especially women's feelings' (p. 104), combine to suggest that she too has a lesbian past.

Finally, the allegorical section about leaving the walled garden alludes to the expulsion of Adam and Eve after eating the forbidden fruit from the Tree of Knowledge. The two sides of the wall can **metaphorically** represent the spiritual and the secular world, but similarly, they can also represent the two choices Jeanette seems to be presented with – heterosexuality or homosexuality. However, the possibility of re-entering the garden is significant and suggests that it is possible to move between the two sides of the wall and to express sexual desire in a more fluid way.

NARRATIVE TECHNIQUE

The story is told in the first person, that is from the point of view of an internal narrator, 'I'. The novel creates the impression of an adult narrator telling the story of her childhood and youth. The child Jeanette's innocent misunderstandings and typically childlike observations are a source of humour, but the more knowing voice of the adult Jeanette comments **ironically** and critically on these events. The use of first person narrative is important in establishing a close relationship between the reader and the central character; indeed, this narrative technique assumes a sympathetic response. It invites the reader to identify with the central character and to engage with her experiences. It is also crucial in guiding our responses since our view of events is restricted to that of the central character. Because we are given insights into Jeanette's thoughts and feelings, we are more likely to accept her comments and interpretations.

From the outset, the first person narration and the humour produced by the child Jeanette's innocence and logic endears the reader to her and her story. This narrative strategy is crucial in disarming any hostility or negative response to her lesbian sexuality as it emerges later. It is also effective in deflecting criticism and antagonism towards the figures of authority – her mother, the pastor and other adult characters – who seek to mould her to fit their own extreme ideas and views of the world. Since Jeanette's lesbianism is central to her identity and experience, it is vitally important that we are willing to take her side.

JUXTAPOSITION OF NARRATIVE ELEMENTS

In the introduction to the novel, Winterson suggests that the narrative structure she employs is compatible with the way the mind works: 'Our mental processes are closer to a maze than a motorway, every turning yields another turning, not symmetrical, not obvious. Not chaos either' (p. xiii). The narrative is non-linear and digressive; it jumps about from topic to topic, with the narrative elements seemingly organised, like the process of thought, by **association** – one idea or memory triggers another similar or connected idea or memory. Although there is an overall chronological movement, time in the novel is also inconsistent and non-linear in places: the narrative leaps a space of seven years and Jeanette's departure and her time away from home is not dealt with at a realist level, but only in the timeless space of the fairy tale and allegorical sections.

The juxtaposition of certain elements does, however, seem significant in terms of influencing interpretation and foreshadowing events. For instance, Jeanette's recollection of the gypsy's prophesy is juxtaposed with her memory of being banned from the paper shop owned by the lesbian couple. In this way, the possibility of Jeanette's own lesbian sexuality is subtly raised. Similarly, the recollection of Jeanette's childhood eavesdropping on the women gossiping about the dissatisfaction of marriage precedes Jeanette and Melanie's first meeting and the development of their lesbian relationship. This organisation of material might help to displace any hostility to the lesbian relationship.

FORM AND STRUCTURE

GENRE

In this novel Winterson blurs the boundaries between realism and fantasy, two modes of writing that are usually seen as opposites. She also seems to be both drawing on and simultaneously undermining traditional genres. Her aim in adopting these techniques is to unsettle our assumptions about what we are reading, to revise the genres so as to accommodate her story of a poor, working-class lesbian, and to make us think. She revises three traditional narrative structures: **autobiographical fiction**, the *Bildungsroman* and the Bible.

REALISM AND FANTASY

In *Oranges* Winterson intersperses realist narrative sections, set in a specific place at a specific time, with timeless allegorical fantasy and fairy-tale elements. **Realism**, with its adherence to linear chronology and **verisimilitude**, she considers to be a restrictive mode of writing because it limits what can be written and imagined. Fantasy and fairy-tale modes open up possibilities, enable an escape from what Winterson calls the 'dull reality of the clock' (Wachtel, in *Malahat Review*, Spring 1997, p. 66). The fantasy mode expresses a desire to overcome constraints and limitations and is 'a more honest reality' because it encompasses the potential of the imagination to move freely in time and to go beyond the physical body and the material world (ibid., p. 67).

In *Oranges* the fantasy and fairy-tale sections mirror and comment on the realist narrative, but also open up an imaginary space, where it is possible for Jeanette to express her desires and ambitions when the realist story threatens to stifle her. The fantasy sections also act as an emotional 'safety valve', creating a space where conflicts can be played out, painful unconscious or repressed feelings can be expressed, and complex and contradictory thoughts externalised. The fantasy sections are crucial for our understanding of the characters, their decisions and motivations for action, which are not fully acknowledged or explicitly voiced by the characters themselves. These non-realist sections explore alternative choices for Jeanette and fill in the gaps of the realist narrative in a metaphorical way. These sections also highlight the idea of storytelling, with its important function of helping us to make sense of the world. Storytelling is subversive, however, in that it counters the idea of an ultimate authority, of one version of truth. The fantasy elements are ambiguous, open to interpretation, and offer a counter to the authority and oppressiveness of Jeanette's mother's polarised view of the world. **Juxtaposing** biblical stories with fairy tales and Arthurian legend also undermines the authority of the Bible in treating it as a set of cultural myths which, like other narrative forms, can be appropriated and revised.

The fairy tales in *Oranges* add humour as well as offering serious messages about conventional gender roles and the need to revise them. Fairy tales are an important cultural form in terms of their psychological and socialising functions. However, many feminist writers have objected that fairy tales perpetuate restrictive gender models for women (the ideals of beauty, passivity and compliance are constantly reinforced) and offer only the severely limited option of marriage as a means of achieving success and happiness. In *Oranges*, Winterson deliberately revises the gender politics of this traditional form; her fairy-tale heroines reject traditional roles and refuse the deceptive option of the romantic 'happy ever after' marriage. She adopts the **rhetorical** device of things in threes in a way that exaggerates this fairy-tale convention, thus humorously exposing the formulaic nature of the plots and **ideological** content.

In the tale of the prince who sought perfection, in Leviticus, the usual romantic pattern is comically undercut. The most beautiful woman is assertive, resourceful and independent; the traditional romance plot comes to an abrupt and unconventional end when she refuses to marry the prince. This tale also exposes the class prejudice of traditional fairy tales; here, moving up the social ladder is not a priority, and the prince himself (with both class and gender privilege) is presented as ridiculous. Similarly, the Winnet tale not only functions as a more light-hearted and ironic version of Jeanette's experience of her mother's powerful manipulation, but also comically revises the fairy-tale form with incongruously contemporary references (to French bread and security systems) and with imagery conventionally associated with the domestic realm and women (a pressure cooker) to describe the traditionally male-dominated public domain of the kingdom. The allegorical fairy tales that explore Jeanette's mother's religious conversion also express the way she would like to idealise her decision. In this way, the real driving force behind her choice, which seems to be the urgent need to satisfy her intense ambition for an influential role, is masked.

AUTOBIOGRAPHICAL FICTION

This novel can be defined as **autobiographical fiction.** The opening sentence parodies the typical beginnings of autobiographical writing, and elements of this story closely resemble elements of Jeanette Winterson's life. Despite the unusual context and experiences the novel is concerned with (extremist religion, coming out as a lesbian, preparing corpses), the ordinariness and universality of this story is stressed from the beginning. However, Winterson does not adhere to the conventions of this genre. Rather, she prompts us to think about genre and the expectations set up by writing in a particular form. She seems deliberately to keep the reader guessing about how much is fiction, how much autobiography and, further, maintains this uncertainty by the use of allegorical fantasy and fairy tales, which disrupt the realist narrative and maintain ambiguity about the 'facts' of the life she is relating.

BILDUNGSROMAN

As several critics have noted (see Part 6), *Oranges* in many ways conforms to the narrative pattern of the *Bildungsroman*, tracing the development of a central character, traditionally a boy, through several rite of passage experiences. Usually at the celebratory end of such narratives the protagonist returns home and assumes his identity and vocation, conforming to the values of his society. However, the ideological implications of this narrative form (the confirmation of the status quo and of conventional gender identities and sexuality) is radically subverted by the model of lesbian girlhood and lesbian coming-out story Winterson creates. The *Bildungsroman* is traditionally narrated in a realist mode, with a knowable, realistic central protagonist who attains an unproblematic, unified sense of identity. The mixing of realist and fantasy elements in Jeanette's development, however, unsettles this notion of identity; Jeanette has several fantasy counterparts and there are multiple versions of her story. The result is that we have a sense of Jeanette's identity as being, to a certain extent, more ambiguous, uncertain and contradictory.

The ending of *Oranges* also departs from the traditional certainty of the *Bildungsroman* in that it remains open and ambiguous; Jeanette hopes to be saved by 'a woman in another place', but this is only a possibility, and the novel ends with her feeling of being displaced and in a state of limbo.

PARODY

Winterson also uses the biblical framework as a structuring device. She takes her chapter titles from the books of the Old Testament and refers in a general way to one or two of the key elements of the biblical stories. Given the subject matter and themes of the novel, this seems an entirely appropriate structure to describe Jeanette's development. However, in adopting this structure, Winterson is also parodying the biblical stories – she is comically reducing this authoritative and sacred text about the history and struggles of a whole people to tell the story of one young woman's life. This rewriting is also subversive – the books of the Bible in this case are used to tell a story that is fundamentally at odds with the conventional heterosexist interpretations of the Bible. She also sends up the fundamentalist literalist interpretations of the Bible and mocks Jeanette's church's way of seeing their ordinary lives in cosmic terms. Thus the revisions of biblical stories and the comic reduction of their perspective on the world undermine the patriarchal authority of the church. However, this appropriation of biblical structure also has political implications in that it enables Winterson to write lesbianism into the Judaeo-Christian tradition, to revise this central cultural text in order to make space for lesbian sexuality.

ALLUSION

This novel makes **allusion** not only to the Bible and fairy tales, but also to a range of other novels, drama, myths, poems and operas, and to specific artists, poets, dramatists, writers and composers. These allusions help to develop the **themes** of the novel, and stress the importance of imagination, vision and storytelling. *Oranges* also alludes to figures who challenged the established social and literary order (Oscar Wilde, for example) and to an obscured lesbian tradition (Charlotte Brontë had a life-long, passionate friendship with Ellen Nussey, which some historians consider to be a lesbian bond; similarly, Christina Rossetti's poem *Goblin Market* is highly erotic and suggestively lesbian). Winterson appropriates, adapts, selects, rewrites, subverts and parodies these references. Jeanette uses such allusion to forge an identity for herself in the face of her mother's imposition of her own expectations about Jeanette's role in life.

The most extensive allusions are made to Malory's *Morte d'Arthur* and Charlotte Brontë's *Jane Eyre*: these texts can be seen as providing a balance to the Bible, a text that pervades every aspect of Jeanette's life. These books create a sense of other realities, which keep her mother's and the church's sense of reality in proportion in what can be called a **dialogic** relationship. Malory drew on existing French romances and other versions of the Arthurian legend for his fifteenth-century retelling of the story of King Arthur's court and the quest for the Holy Grail (see p. 27). Unlike the earlier sources, however, the emphasis in Malory's version was on a clash of loyalties within a group of people rather than on the spiritual/secular division, as in other versions. At the point in *Oranges* when the Sir Perceval sections appear, Jeanette's conflict with her mother has moved on from a clash over belief to a more deeply painful and complex antagonism, bound up with a sense of immense loss and betrayal, as well as love and a longing to return home.

Critic Tess Cosslett considers *Jane Eyre* to be a significant **intertext** for Jeanette's story of development for a number of reasons. There are similarities in terms of plot (the troubled romance and quest for self-discovery) and themes (love and exile); the narrative that ends with Jane's return to a blind, maimed and hence 'feminised' Rochester as his financial, emotional and physical equal is, Cosslett suggests, 'a tempered and redefined romance' (in *Postmodern Studies 25*, eds Grice and Woods, p. 24). This obviously has resonance with Jeanette's own redefinition of romance between women. The treatment of *Jane Eyre* in *Oranges* is also significant because it highlights the way her mother forces everything to conform to her own view of the world, as well as her revisionary tendencies (which Jeanette learns). It is also important because it becomes a **symbol** of her mother's betrayal after Jeanette discovers the real ending of the novel.

HUMOUR

Oranges is undoubtedly a funny novel; its clever wit and comic episodes have enchanted readers and critics from the outset. The child Jeanette's innocent misunderstandings and naïve perspective, and the **irony** and cutting ridicule of the knowing older narrator are significant sources of humour. The revisionary perspective offered by the parody of biblical stories produces a comic effect, as does the ridiculing of authority figures in the church. However, humour has a serious and subversive role in this novel too; it is used to undermine prejudice and to enable painful issues to be expressed. Humour endears us to Jeanette and the ridicule of the church members as power-obsessed, narrow-minded and extremist alienates us from their views and undermines their authority. Wit and laughter work to upturn conventional responses and to disrupt hierarchies of value, causing a reassessment of the way we judge and altering the way we interpret the world and others. As critic Isabel C. Anievas Gamallo suggests, 'Laughter...remains a politically subversive weapon that challenges conventional standards of perceiving and writing the world' (in *The Girl: Constructions of the Girl in Contemporary Fiction by Women*, ed. Saxton, pp. 125–6).

LANGUAGE AND STYLE

Winterson takes language very seriously; she considers it vital that writers continue to develop language as a tool for expression and communication of powerful emotions: it 'is the preserve of poetry and of true fiction, to put down roots through the surface, down into the subsoil of the human heart and to draw up those elements that would otherwise lie locked there, unheard, unspoken, perhaps unregarded' (Wachtel, in *Malahat Review*, Spring 1994, p. 64). She considers language to be important not only because it explains the world, but because it shapes reality. It can bring freedom or it can limit experience and perception. Being immersed in biblical language and the fundamentalist **discourse** of the church determines Jeanette's perception and experience of the world: 'I learned to interpret the signs and wonders that the unbeliever might never understand' (p. 17). At school her language and frame of reference are at odds with those of the other children and she is left ostracised and confused. One of the key turning points in the novel is when Jeanette finally leaves home and begins to see the world no longer filtered through the dramatic fundamentalist discourse of her mother and the church: 'It was not judgement day, but another morning' (p. 134).

Throughout the novel, Winterson is engaged in a parody of the Bible, and comically alludes to specific biblical events and phrases in order undermine the authority of her mother and the church. Her mother's sense of the god-ordained necessity of adopting Jeanette, for instance, is sent up by the use of phrases that echo the story of the Nativity: 'a star came to settle over an orphanage, and in that place was a crib, and in that crib, a child. A child with too much hair' (p. 10). The mythical qualities and sense of gravity created by the biblical echoes is comically undercut by the banal fact that the child has too much hair. Similarly, the mechanical effect of 'She would get a child, train it, build it, dedicate it to the Lord' undermines any sense of her mother's actions being a profound expression of her devotion. Fundamentalist literalist interpretations of the Bible are also treated with **irony** in many places throughout the novel.

However, Winterson also on occasion mimics the Bible's **rhetoric** and momentous style, creating the sense of a prophet-like utterance in order to convey the power and deeply felt passion of certain moments. For example, immediately after the comic send-up of Jeanette's mother's aspirations, there is a short passage that creates a sense of suspended time: 'We stood on the hill and my mother said, "This world is full of sin." We stood on the hill and my mother said, "You can change the world"' (p. 10). The simple repetition and biblical rhetoric give her mother's words a momentous quality and encapsulate her mother's strongly held beliefs. Similarly, the phrase 'And it was evening and it was morning; another day', which is used to describe Jeanette and Melanie's first sexual experience, also echoes biblical phrasing in order to convey the profound nature of their experience.

Winterson's use of different kinds of language or **registers** is wide and inclusive. Her narrative shifts between biblical language, philosophical statements, fairy-tale phrases, gossip in the **vernacular**, nursery rhymes and elusively metaphorical passages, with metaphors sometimes becoming literalised in a **magic realist** way. This kind of

plurality in language use has been called 'dialogic', with each mode of speaking being 'in dialogue' with the others. If language can control our perception and understanding of the world, and can determine our notion of reality, the effect of this plurality is that there is no one version of the truth, no one reality; our experience can have only a relative meaning. This emphasis on the relative nature of experience and reality is important to the novel as a whole and to Jeanette's departure from the limitations imposed by the absolutist world view on which the church and Jeanette's mother insist. A plurality of voices and ways of seeing the world disrupts the unwavering certainty of the church, a certainty that has its basis in the rigid hierarchy of **binary oppositions** which structure their response to experience.

PART FOUR

TEXTUAL ANALYSIS

TEXT 1   (PAGES 3–4)

Like most people I lived for a long time with my mother and father. My father liked to watch the wrestling, my mother liked to wrestle; it didn't matter what. She was in the white corner and that was that.

She hung out the largest sheets on the windiest days. She *wanted* the Mormons to knock on the door. At election time in a Labour mill town she put a picture of the Conservative candidate in the window.

She had never heard of mixed feelings. There were friends and there were enemies.

Enemies were: The Devil (in his many forms)

Next Door

Sex (in its many forms)

Slugs

Friends were: God

Our dog

Aunty Madge

The Novels of Charlotte Brontë

Slug pellets

and me, at first. I had been brought in to join her in a tag match against the Rest of the World. She had a mysterious attitude to the begetting of children; it wasn't that she couldn't do it, more that she didn't want to do it. She was very bitter about the Virgin Mary getting there first. So she did the next best thing and arranged for a foundling. That was me.

I cannot recall a time when I did not know that I was special. We had no Wise Men because she didn't believe there were any wise men, but we had sheep. One of my earliest memories is me sitting on a sheep at Easter while she told me the story of the Sacrificial Lamb. We had it on Sundays with potato.

This opening is important for a number of reasons. Its deadpan humour sets the tone for the rest of the novel and immediately engages the reader's interest, as does the first person narration. We get a strong sense of Jeanette's mother's personality and outlook on life, a sense of the mother–daughter relationship, the environment in which Jeanette grows up, and information about Jeanette's adoption.

The opening sentence parodies the typical beginnings of autobiographical writing and raises questions of genre, which continue to be teased out as the novel progresses. It also suggests that the novel will deal with common or typical issues about growing up in a nuclear family, although this reading is countered by the specific context that is then revealed. Both universal and more context-specific readings of this novel abound. The first person narration and colloquial style invite the reader to identify with Jeanette, an important factor in the success of the novel, given the hostility that homosexuality can provoke and given the novel's attacks on the church. In this opening section and throughout the chapters concerned with Jeanette's childhood, typically childlike observations and logic are a source of humour and effectively endear the reader to Jeanette and her story. However, as in other **autobiographical fiction** where an adult narrator tells his/her life story retrospectively, there is a dual narrative voice – that of the innocent child and that of the more knowing adult narrator whose narration, in this case, comments ironically and critically on these earlier events.

This dual narration is apparent here, where the scathing mockery of Jeanette's mother's dogmatic, narrow-minded views is expressed through a typically childlike list of friends and enemies. The curious mixture of items on the list ranges from those with obvious, serious moral implications – God and the Devil – to more trivial friends and enemies – slug pellets and slugs. The incongruity of the list has a comic effect and seems to reflect Jeanette's childish view of the world, where she is unable to distinguish a hierarchy of seriousness or importance. However, as we learn more of Jeanette's mother, we might decide that actually this list does accurately reflect her own, often petty, vengeance against a whole range of things that hinder her or contradict her views. This eclectic list suggests the wide-ranging nature of Jeanette's mother's sense of anger and vengeance; her antagonism finds vent at all levels and in all areas – cosmic, political, religious, personal and even in the garden.

The arrangement of these items under the oppositional categories, friends and enemies, also highlights her mother's antagonistic attitude. From the outset of the novel, then, her absolutist and polarised world view is the target for mockery, and her pride, vanity and belligerent narrow-mindedness are all treated with irony. Her confrontational attitude is demonstrated by the fact that she '*wanted* the Mormons to knock on the door' so that she can argue with them, the italics emphasising her enthusiasm for conflict. Similarly, announcing her Conservative politics is bound to provoke hostility in a manufacturing town loyal to the socialist politics of the old Labour Party.

Describing her extremist sense of being at war with the world in terms of a 'tag match' again presents her mother's sense of antagonism through an appropriate childlike frame of reference. Simultaneously, such description, in conjunction with the capitalisation of the 'Rest of the World', trivialises the massive scale on which her mother sees her struggle to assert her religious convictions and her unquestionable sense of what is right in the face of what she perceives as the immense heathen opposition. Her inability to have 'mixed feelings', her polarised response to experience and her apparently volatile temperament do not bode well for Jeanette. Significantly, not only are we told that Jeanette was on her mother's list of friends only 'at first', but the layout of the text reinforces Jeanette's relegation, inevitably to the list of enemies; Jeanette's 'me' has literally been forced off the end of the list. This subtle anticipation of the plot to come prepares the reader for mother–daughter conflict.

This demotion of Jeanette also reveals much about what determines the definition of either friend or enemy. As the later revelations of Jeanette's mother's revision and truncation of *Jane Eyre* reveals, the location of an item or person on her list of friends is entirely dependent on how far they can be forced to conform to Jeanette's mother's world view. Jeanette can remain on her mother's list of friends only as long as she conforms to her mother's plan for her to become a missionary. As long as she does this, she is considered and feels herself to be 'special'. Possibly, the key element that shocks Jeanette later, when her relationship with Melanie is discovered and condemned as sinful, is the contradiction of her sense of having a special calling and of being, without question, one of the righteous.

Her mother's desire for power and influence is also laid open to mockery here. The church is an arena which not only allows her to assert her views with authority, but which will also give her scope to follow her ambitions. The extent of her ambition borders on the blasphemous and is mockingly described in terms of her bitterness that the Virgin Mary was the first woman to achieve fame, recognition and sainthood by being the virgin mother of Jesus. There is much irony directed against Jeanette's mother due to the implicit comparison of her ruthless impatience, selfishness and belligerence with the qualities of patience and sympathy for human suffering for which the Virgin Mary is beloved. Other allusions to the Nativity parody the Biblical story and further highlight and mock her mother's absolutist views: 'We had no Wise Men because she didn't believe there were any wise men, but we had sheep.' Similarly, the literalist approach to the Bible is comically undermined by the childlike connection Jeanette makes between the Sacrificial Lamb (see p. 15) and Sunday dinner. These methods of undermining the authority of the Bible and of her mother's views are typical of the novel as a whole.

These opening paragraphs offer a tightly packed and mocking 'snapshot' of Jeanette's mother, using humour to endear us to Jeanette and to encourage us to sympathise with her in the face of her mother's domineering and belligerent nature. In many ways she is a positive role model for Jeanette, proving that women can be strong, powerful and pursue their ambitions. However, the violence implicit in her attitudes and in her usurping of what are traditionally considered masculine attributes of open and active confrontation (effectively conveyed in the **metaphor** of wrestling) introduce a note of discomfort and trepidation about the consequences for Jeanette of no longer being on her mother's list of friends.

TEXT *2*   (PAGES 27–8)

> I sniffed; disinfectant and mashed potatoes. Then my mother prodded me, put her
> letter on the bedside cabinet, and emptied a huge carrier bag of oranges into the
> bowl by my water jug. I smiled feebly, hoping to gain support, but instead she
> patted me on the head and rolled away. So I was alone. I thought of Jane Eyre,
> who faced many trials and was always brave. My mother read the book to me
> whenever she felt sad; she said it gave her fortitude. I picked up her letter: the
> usual not-to-worry, lots-of-people-will-visit, chin-up, and a promise to work hard
> on the bathroom, and not let Mrs White get in the way. That she'd come soon, or

if not she'd send her husband. That my operation would be the next day. At this, I let the letter fall to the bed. The next day! What if I died? So young and so promising! I thought of my funeral, of all the tears. I wanted to be buried with Golly and my Bible. Should I write instructions? Could I count on any of them to take any notice? My mother knew all about illness and operations. The doctor had told her that a woman in her condition shouldn't be walking around, but she said that her time hadn't come, and at least she knew where she was going, not like him. My mother read in a book that more people die under anaesthetic than drown while water-skiing.

'If the Lord brings you back,' she told May, before she went in for her gallstones, 'you'll know it's because he's got work for you to do.' I crept under the bedclothes and prayed to be brought back.

On the morning of my operation, the nurses were smiling and rearranging the bed again, and piling the oranges in a symmetrical tower. Two hairy arms lifted me up and strapped me on to a cold trolley. The castors squeaked and the man who pushed me went too fast. Corridors, double doors and two pairs of eyes peeping over the top of tight white masks. A nurse held my hand while someone fitted a muzzle over my nose and mouth. I breathed in and saw a great line of water-skiers falling off and not coming back up. Then I didn't see anything at all.

'Jelly, Jeanette.'

I *knew* it, I'd died and the angels were giving me jelly. I opened my eyes expecting to see a pair of wings.

'Come on, eat up,' the voice encouraged.

'Are you an angel?' I asked hopefully.

'Not quite, I'm a doctor. But she's an angel, aren't you nurse?'

The angel blushed.

'I can hear,' I said, to no one in particular.

'Eat your jelly,' said the nurse.

After Miss Jewsbury has forced Jeanette's mother to get medical attention for Jeanette's deafness, the child is immediately admitted to hospital. When her mother returns to the hospital with her pyjamas, she offers Jeanette little comfort, merely writing a letter to her explaining that she is to have an operation the following day and then leaving her alone. The whole experience causes Jeanette to reassess her trust in the certainty of the church's views; their interpretation of her condition in evangelical terms, as being filled with the Holy Spirit, is proved wrong by the medical authority. What she feels as her mother's abandonment forces her to try to find comfort and her own explanation of this frightening experience. It is written from the child Jeanette's point of view, so, like many of the chapters dealing with her childhood, it is comic. However, the fear and trauma that this comedy masks is also made apparent.

As always, Jeanette's mother offers little maternal care, nor can she empathise with her daughter's fears at this point. She rarely touches Jeanette, and here 'prodded' her to point out the letter she had written and then merely 'patted' her before she leaves, despite Jeanette's appeal for support. She brings oranges, her customary substitute for maternal love, here a carrier bagful, and then, with apparent ease and self-confidence, 'rolled' away. The short, blunt sentence 'So I was alone' is melodramatic but sums up the complete isolation Jeanette feels in the alien environment of the children's ward. The decoration designed for children merely makes her feel uncomfortable, and she is at the mercy of adults who deny her the pleasure of playing with plasticine, despite her logical argument about its safety.

However, Jeanette is determined, resourceful and imaginative, and tries to comfort herself by thinking of her mother's favourite novel, *Jane Eyre*. In thinking of a novel that her mother says gives her 'fortitude', Jeanette is seeking a substitute source of comfort. The letter her mother leaves does not reassure Jeanette; her summing up of its contents in terms of empty clichéd phrases, 'the usual not-to-worry, lots-of-people-will-visit, chin-up', stresses her mother's lack of concern. Her distance and apparent lack of interest in Jeanette's traumatic situation is stressed by her half-hearted promise to visit, which is conditional on her progress with the bathroom. This lack of involvement and emotional distance in her personal relationships is iterated by the fact that if she could not come, she would 'send her husband'. Equally, referring to her father as her mother's 'husband' could be an expression of Jeanette's sense of her father's insignificance in terms of his influence in the family or as a potential source of support.

Jeanette's response to the letter is presented in humorously **melodramatic** terms, with questions and exclamation marks comically punctuating her elaborate chain of thought about her funeral. However, despite the wit and lightness with which this response is handled, the question that triggers it is also very serious for Jeanette at this point: 'What if I died?' In a way typical of a child, Jeanette plans to be buried with her soft toy. However, her doubt about whether anyone will pay any attention to her wishes reinforces our recognition that Jeanette has little say in what she does and that, despite her confident self-assertion, she is vulnerable and powerless.

This vulnerability is emphasised in her experience of being taken down to the operating theatre. Although the child's point of view is humorous here – it is not a male nurse who lifts her on to the stretcher trolley but 'Two hairy arms' – we also get a sense of Jeanette's fear, discomfort and powerlessness to escape. She is 'strapped' on to 'a cold trolley' which is pushed 'too fast'. The quick succession of 'Corridors, double doors and two pairs of eyes' conveys the apparent speed with which she arrives at the operating theatre, thus creating a sense of her panic, but also suggesting her lack of control – all she can do is observe what she sees from her position lying on the stretcher trolley. That she sees only 'two pairs of eyes peeping over the top of tight white masks' is what we might expect in this situation, but again the impersonality, even dehumanisation, of the surgeons adds to Jeanette's fear. Her description of the 'muzzle' that is 'fitted' over her nose and mouth suggests her inexperience, as she draws on a familiar word to describe something unfamiliar. It also again suggests her sense of powerlessness, since a muzzle would be associated in Jeanette's experience with the control of a dog. Although the nurse holds her hand, presumably to reassure her, Jeanette could equally interpret this as further restraint.

Throughout this experience Jeanette has been desperately trying to remember anything about medical issues and operations which might help her to understand what is happening or offer comfort. However, the things she can recall do not help. As the anaesthetic takes effect, her fears of death are expressed in terms of what she recalls of her mother's authoritative views on the dangers of anaesthetic. The somewhat strained comparison between the number of people who die under anaesthetic and the number who drown while water-skiing, which forms the statistical evidence for her views, ironically undermines the validity of her opinion. However, it does fuel Jeanette's fears: 'I breathed in and saw a great line of water-skiers falling off and not coming back up.' Similarly, she remembers her mother's words of 'comfort' to May before she had an operation to remove her gallstones, and prays to be brought back from the anaesthetic to do God's work.

When she wakes up, she is convinced she has died and gone to heaven. Her child's point of view on what heaven would be like – with jelly readily available – is amusing. However, the return of her sense of certainty – she '*knew*' she'd gone to heaven – is compromised by the context in which she finds herself. Playing out the clichéd romantic flirtation between doctors and nurses, the doctor examining Jeanette does concur with Jeanette's perception of the nurse at least as an 'angel'. However, this also highlights the different meanings 'angel' can have in different contexts. Jeanette's concept of 'angel' is influenced by the religious context in which she has learnt it; in this context, however, it is a term of romantic flirtation and a sentimental term to describe nurses. Although Jeanette does not consciously realise it, her way of seeing the world in her mother's absolutist terms is gradually changing, and Elsie's influence in the week that follows Jeanette's operation fuels this process of change.

TEXT 3   (PAGES 86–7)

> When I reached Melanie's it was getting dark. I had to cut through the churchyard to get there, and sometimes I'd steal her a bunch of flowers from the new graves. She was always pleased, but then, I never told her where they came from. She asked me if I wanted to stay overnight because her mum was away and she didn't like being in the house on her own. I said I'd ring a neighbour, and after much trouble finally got an agreement from my mother, who had to be fetched from her lettuces. We read the Bible as usual, and then told each other how glad were that the Lord had brought us together. She stroked my head for a long time, and then we hugged and it felt like drowning. Then I was frightened but couldn't stop. There was something crawling in my belly. I had an octopus inside me.
>
> And it was evening and it was morning; another day.

After that we did everything together, and I stayed with her as often as I could. My mother seemed relieved that I was seeing less of Graham, and for a while made no mention of the amount of time I spent with Melanie.

'Do you think this is Unnatural Passion?' I asked her once.

'Doesn't feel like it. According to Pastor Finch, that's awful.'

She must be right, I thought.

Melanie and I had volunteered to set up the Harvest Festival Banquet, and we worked hard in the church throughout the day. When everyone arrived and started to pass the potato pie, we stood on the balcony, looking down on them. Our family. It was safe.

Here is a table set for a feast, and the guests are arguing about the best recipe for goose. Now and again a tremor shakes the chandelier, dropping tiny flakes of plaster into the sherbet. The guests look up more in interest than alarm. It's cold in here, very cold. The women suffer most. Their shoulders bared and white like hard-boiled eggs. Outside, under the snow, the river lies embalmed. These are the elect, and in the hall an army sleeps on straw.

Outside a rush of torches.

Laughter drifts into the hall. The elect have always been this way.

Getting old, dying, starting again. Not noticing.

Father and Son. Father and Son.

It has always been this way, nothing can intrude.

Father, Son and Holy Ghost.

Outside, the rebels Storm the Winter Palace.

This passage marks a huge turning point in Jeanette and Melanie's relationship, which, after what seems to have been a gradual increase in intimacy, becomes sexual. Both the realist and fantasy sections signal danger and use **dramatic irony** to warn of the devastation to come. As in many other parts of the novel, the fantasy section here metaphorically echoes the realist narrative and anticipates the plot development. As in the rest of the novel, the **juxtaposition** of narrative elements is significant to our understanding of the more subtle, not explicitly articulated, shifts in feeling.

Jeanette's gesture of giving flowers to Melanie is typically romantic and suggests that their relationship has been slowly and gently progressing towards increasing intimacy. The necessity of stealing the flowers from the churchyard at once reminds us of Jeanette's lack of money, and suggests a recklessness and disrespect for the dead born out of her desire to please the woman she loves. Their relationship is entirely bound up with the church and they use the Bible and the focus of their faith in order to express their happiness at becoming close. It seems that their expression of intimacy in this way is a means of affirming a bond which they have no language to express. The ritual of reading the Bible and reconfirming their bond in terms of their happiness in their faith can be read as a displaced expression of the feelings they have for one another, which are harder to understand and impossible to articulate.

On this particular evening, however, their tentative sensual contact, as Melanie strokes Jeanette's hair, becomes more physical. Jeanette experiences their hug as something overwhelming, suggesting an outpouring of unacknowledged or unrealised desires. She feels as if she is 'drowning', and although afraid of this unknown experience, she is unable to halt the momentum of her passionate response. The intensity of the emotion and sexual arousal she feels, but is unable to control, is suitably expressed via the **metaphor** of the octopus 'crawling' in her belly. This **image** effectively conveys both the physical and emotional feelings she is experiencing, which seem to have taken her over.

The single-sentence paragraph about the passing of the night is effective in conveying the sense of Jeanette and Melanie being unaware of time, lost in the moment of the profound and life-changing experience of realising their passion for one another and acting on their desires. It is also a reference to the Book of Genesis, conveying the idea of a new birth, and carries the momentous weight of this biblical allusion and also the sense of timelessness that so much of the Bible expresses. It refuses to ground this experience in explicit realist detail, but rather elevates it to create a sense of its immense significance. Crucially, it reconfirms the way that Jeanette and Melanie see their lesbian desire as being firmly within the bounds of their faith, a certainty that is subtly put into doubt by Jeanette detecting hints of her mother's suspicion.

There is irony in Jeanette's mother's relief that she is seeing less of Graham. Presumably she thinks that Jeanette is now safe from possible distraction from the life of celibate missionary she has planned for her. However, we are alerted to the possibility of Jeanette's mother's suspicion by the subtle suggestion that, although she made no mention of the time spent with Melanie 'for a while', she did at some point draw attention to it. The juxtaposition of this hint with Jeanette's questioning of the definition of her relationship with Melanie suggests that Jeanette's own tentative doubts about the legitimacy of their relationship within the church has been in part triggered by her mother's comments. However, Jeanette and Melanie rapidly rule out the possibility of their feelings being Unnatural Passions because they experience their desire as both good and natural. Their innocence and trust in the faith that has brought them together and enabled their relationship to develop sets up a tension caused by dramatic irony – the reader can see that their relationship is precisely what the church will define as Unnatural Passions and demon-possession. They work together to organise the Harvest Festival Banquet, and their commitment and feelings of being wholly secure and of belonging to their church family only serve to increase the reader's sense of foreboding for the events that will inevitably follow.

The brief allegorical tale metaphorically warns of the extent of the damage to come. It refers obliquely to an historical event – the storming of the Winter Palace during the Russian Revolution and the overthrow of the old aristocratic order. The setting of the tale is a banquet for the elect, an obvious parallel to the Harvest Festival Banquet for the church congregation. The elect are complacently secure in their sense of the order and pattern of their lives. The repetition of 'Father and Son' represents the cyclical patterns of life and death, and the ongoing and seemingly eternal perpetuation of **patriarchal** power through male inheritance in the secular world. The phrase also obviously refers to, and in this short tale is extended into, the Christian trinity of 'Father Son and Holy Ghost'. The sense is that this order is inevitable and eternal at both a secular and spiritual level.

The mention of 'recipes for goose' recalls the fairy tale in Leviticus, where the goose is punished for dissent from the Prince's/ church's views. Jeanette has already discovered that in the male-dominated secular world women 'suffer most', and she is about to discover that this is the case for the world of the patriarchal church as well. The female elect are the most affected by the cold of the hall, their feminine gowns leaving them open to the cold. The mundane and domestic simile likening their shoulders to hard-boiled eggs squashes any notion that their gendered dress and social position is either romantic or desirable. The coldness of the hall symbolically suggests the frozen, static and life-denying order that dominates this world. Outside, the river, symbol of life, is also frozen over, metaphorically 'embalmed'.

The tale reinforces Jeanette and Melanie's innocence about how their relationship will be seen; like them, the elect feel secure within their palace and only look in interest when a tremor shakes the chandelier. However, the tiny flakes of plaster that ruin the sherbet are hints of the devastation to follow, hints that also echo those in the realist narrative noticed but disregarded by Jeanette. The slight incongruity of the specific naming of the dessert as sherbet adds a note of lightness, which serves to contrast with the mounting sense of tension. Neither Jeanette nor the elect are troubled, but these hints foretell of the chaos that is imminent. Just as the army sleeps comfortably, its defences down, and the elect remain unaware of the trouble mounting in the world outside the Winter Palace, neither the congregation, not Jeanette and Melanie are aware of the radical upheaval that lies ahead.

However, this **allegory** does not simply suggest that Jeanette and Melanie are the rebels about to storm the palace. On the contrary, at this point they see themselves very much as insiders, as part of the elect, secure in their position within the palace/church. In fact it is only ever the elect/leaders of the church who, perceiving their lesbianism as a powerful threat to their patriarchal order, define them as rebels. This allegory suggests that it is the inability of the church to accommodate change, to unfreeze some of its rigid and outdated attitudes, that forces Jeanette and Melanie outside the palace/church and into being the rebels outside.

This allegory picks up and expands on the subtle hints of trouble given in the realist narrative, but it also foreshadows future events, as well as maintaining our sympathy for Jeanette and Melanie in their innocence of what the church will see as their sin.

PART FIVE

Background

THE AUTHOR AND HER WORKS

Jeanette Winterson was born in 1959 and grew up in a working-class home in Accrington, Lancashire. She was adopted by Constance and Jack Winterson, members of a Pentecostal evangelical church. She wrote sermons and preached from an early age, and her parents planned a missionary life for her. She attributes her skilful manipulation of what she calls the 'fabulous tool' and the 'extremely sensitive instrument' of language to this early training and environment, 'I learned how to handle language and the spoken word, and I learned how to persuade. That's what preachers do' (Wachtel, in *Malahat Review*, Spring 1997, pp. 64, 63). There were few books in Winterson's childhood home, only *Jane Eyre* and Malory's retelling of the Arthurian legends, apart from the Bible, but she satisfied her appetite for reading at the local public library. She left home at sixteen after she had begun a relationship with another young woman. She had a number of temporary jobs – at a funeral parlour, selling ice-cream and in a psychiatric hospital. She later went to Accrington College, and then, in 1978, to St Catherine's College, Oxford, to study English. After university, she worked at the Roundhouse Theatre in London, wrote advertising copy, then worked as an editor at Brilliance Books and at the feminist Pandora Press. Her employers at Pandora encouraged her to write *Oranges*, and subsequently published it. She also wrote for the *Sunday Times* and the *Guardian*.

These facts of her life correspond to the realist narrative of *Oranges*, a novel that seems to invite a reading as fictionalised autobiography or a *roman à clef*, especially given that the central character is called Jeanette. Even the fairy-tale and allegorical elements, which disrupt a straightforward interpretation of the novel in these realist terms, seem also suggestively autobiographical – Winnet Stonejar is a near-anagram of the author's name, for instance. However, Winterson has repeatedly refuted the reading of her writing in terms of her life; in *Art Objects: Essays on Ecstasy and Effrontery* she claims: 'It seems to me that the intersection between a writer's life and a writer's work is irrelevant to the reader. The reader is not being offered a chunk of the writer or a direct insight into the writer's mind, the reader is being offered a separate reality (p. 26).'

She also asserts that 'Art must resist autobiography if it hopes to cross the boundaries of class, culture...and...sexuality (ibid., p. 106). She turns the tables on autobiographical readings of *Oranges* by suggesting that it is 'a fiction masquerading as a memoir' (ibid., p. 53). In *Oranges* itself the Deuteronomy chapter refutes the notion that stories or history can convey an objective truth – again, seemingly pointing to the futility of reading this novel as Winterson's personal history. It is a text that blurs boundaries between fact and fiction and between generic forms, realism and fantasy; it is at once, as one critic suggests, a 'multi-layered self-portrait' (Gamallo, in *The Girl*, ed. Saxton, p. 134), but also 'only art and *lies*'.

Winterson's upbringing, immersed in Pentecostal evangelism, has had an influence on her writing in terms of content and style. Her intimate knowledge of the Bible, its stories, metaphorical structures and symbols, linguistic phrasing and rhythms has inspired her passion for language, for harnessing and developing the power of words. As she says, 'For me, language is a freedom' (Wachtel, in *Malahat Review*, Spring, 1997, p. 64). For her the Bible is a source of myth and counter-myth, as her explicit revisions and retellings of biblical stories attest. Her first two novels, *Oranges* and *Boating for Beginners* (1985), offer parodies of biblical stories and criticise the way that systems of belief impact on individuals. Like *Oranges*, *Boating for Beginners* is an irreverent and comic retelling of biblical myth – specifically the story of Noah and his ark. God, in this revision, is one of Noah's failed experiments in creating a superior life form, and religion merely an explanation of this creature's existence. Giving this story a setting of advanced commercial capitalism and mass media, with Noah set to make a fortune from the bestselling collaborations with God on the first of a series of books explaining human history, it is not only biblical authority, but also the powerful cultural machinery of capitalism that comes under scrutiny. The Flood is a result of God's moodiness, and although it was meant to wipe out all but Noah's family, a group of women also survive. They leave behind evidence that counters Noah's deliberately misleading clues about the pre-Flood era. As in *Oranges*, this raises the issue of **plural** perspectives and alternative versions of stories and events.

Storytelling is an important element of Winterson's work. Stories, she suggests, are crucial because they help us to make sense of the world and of ourselves. They can offer security and also a means of escape from restrictions imposed by cultural conventions and limited frames of reference (such as the literalism of fundamentalist religion in *Oranges*). In several interviews Winterson attests to what she feels is the vital importance of stories and the process of storytelling in her own life. Especially when she was a child she used books to 'mark out a charmed place and to save my soul' from the decisions imposed upon her ('My Hardback Heaven', the *Independent Magazine*, 13 June 1995) and felt that 'Books...were kinetic forces. They did not write down the world, they altered it forever' ('Better Than Sex', the *Guardian*, 22 July 1992). In *Oranges*, stories are crucial to Jeanette's development and to her sense of identity. However, the stories imposed upon her are countered by non-biblical stories as she struggles against the life mapped out for her by her mother. The idea that all stories, regardless of the cultural authority they carry, can be challenged, questioned and imagined otherwise is a liberating and empowering one. Imagination in Winterson's fiction is a crucial way of transcending restrictive social codes and conventions, and of resisting culturally constructed ways of perceiving and ordering the world, which are shaped and determined by the institutions of heterosexuality, marriage, the family and the church. The notion of history as a set of stories and not an objective truth is a recurrent element in Winterson's writing, as is the self-conscious reference to the process of storytelling.

Winterson's third novel, *The Passion* (1986), which won the John Llewellyn Rhys Memorial Prize, takes the rise and fall of Napoleon as its historical framework. Through the two first person narratives of Henri, a French peasant who becomes Napoleon's dedicated cook, and Villanelle, the daughter of a Venetian boatman, it offers alternative perspectives on this historical period. The refrain 'Trust me, I'm telling you stories' is a **metafictional** device, drawing attention to the fictionality of the text. It is also an ambiguous phrase, both reassuring and putting into doubt the extent to which we should believe and trust in the stories we are offered. As in *Oranges*, the boundaries between reality and fantasy are blurred, though in a more seamless way, a technique termed **magic realism**. Magic realist moments occur at points of emotional intensity, which can only be expressed in a fantastical mode, at points where feelings seem to transform or go beyond the realistically possible or rationally acceptable. For example, Villanelle literally as well as metaphorically loses her heart to her lover, the Queen of Spades, and engages Henri's help in the quest to retrieve it from where it is kept beating in a jar. Similarly, she literally has the webbed feet mythically associated with Venetian boatmen. As in all of Winterson's fiction, this novel offers a revisionary critique of conventional constructions of gender and sexuality; gender categories are blurred as Henri and Villanelle exhibit traits typically associated with their opposite gender (Henri is sensitive and gentle, Villanelle adventurous and daring), and sexuality is fluid, ambiguous and complex (Villanelle and her lover are both married, and Villanelle also conceives a child by Henri). Lesbian passion is central, but located within a patriarchal social order in which heterosexuality is compulsory. Like *Oranges*, this novel is about obsession and, as in much of Winterson's fiction, about the powerful force field of desire.

Sexing the Cherry (1989) won the E.M. Forster Award from the American Academy of Arts. Again, it takes a specific historical framework (seventeenth-century London, the English Civil War, the Plague and the Great Fire of London) and tells the story of a gargantuan female called Dog Woman, and her foundling son, Jordan, who becomes an explorer. Jordan's struggle to overcome the powerful influence of his fiercely independent adoptive mother is reminiscent of Jeanette's similar struggle. Winterson's experiment with form in this novel is more radical than in previous fiction. The narrative is more digressive, interweaving feminist revisions of fairy tales and shifts in time. Like *The Passion*, the narrative is split between the two first person narratives of Dog Woman and Jordan, thus offering a dual perspective. Notions of identity as something knowable and fixed are undermined by the multiple identities implied by the shifts in time – each seventeenth-century character has a twentieth-century counterpart. Such shifts also raise questions about the nature of reality – it too is something relative, created within a cultural framework determined by a society's beliefs, and not natural or unproblematic. Like Winterson's other novels, *Sexing the Cherry* takes the point of view of outsiders, figures marginalised because they do not conform to the cultural norms of gender or sexuality. It is thus able to offer a critique of the mainstream from this different perspective.

Written on the Body (1992) similarly offers a critique of typical romantic tragedy through its telling of a familiar story of passionate love between the narrator and a married woman, Louise, who develops cancer. However, the novel puts gender stereotypes into question even as it employs them, by refusing to determine the sex of the narrator. The reader cannot be certain whether this is a clichéd heterosexual romance, or an ironic and revisionary lesbian appropriation of the conventions of such familiar narrative forms. Generic expectations are not satisfied, and in this way the effect of generic conventions on the process of interpretation is exposed. As well as more conventional narrative sections, this novel contains fragmented, metafictional passages, where the plot halts and the narrator focuses on each part of the body, making reference to the changes the cancer will bring to Louise's body. These sections use scientific and lyrical language, with echoes of the biblical Song of Solomon. Like other novels, it is concerned with undermining certainties, with issues of identity and the body, and with how language can be used adequately to express the power of desire. This novel met with a mixed critical response. During the early 1990s, Winterson's increasingly experimental writing, in conjunction with her reputation for self-promotion, antagonised and alienated some critics, reviewers and readers, compounding a sense that both she and her writing were becoming increasingly pretentious. Notably, she chose *Written on the Body* as the best book of the year in the 1992 *Daily Telegraph* survey, and in 1994 in the *Sunday Times* she claimed that she was the greatest living writer in the English language – either a display of consummate arrogance or a mockery of the literary establishment.

Art and Lies: A Piece for Three Voices and a Bard (1994) is radically experimental in form; it collapses past and present, as time shifts between the ancient Greek past of the poet Sappho and the (then) slightly futuristic London of about 2000. It has few plot elements linking the three speaking voices of Sappho, a female painter called Picasso, and Handel, a defrocked priest and doctor, and employs passages in Latin and musical scores. All three characters are somehow scarred and/or emotionally traumatised by the family, the church or the literary establishment – Handel has been castrated by a priest, Picasso raped by her half-brother, and Sappho's poetry mutilated and mostly lost. Each figure reflects on his/her endurance of being at odds with society, and for these marginalised characters art becomes the significant means of self-expression. The exploration of the connection between sexuality and artistic expression, and between self-perception and the cultural conventions that in part determine this, is brought to the fore.

In *Gut Symmetries* (1997), Winterson tells the story of a triangular love affair between Alice and a married couple, Stella and Jove; all three narrate the story, which shifts between times and places. As with all of Winterson's fiction, this novel is rich in allusion and draws particularly on the language, concepts and theories of physics, ancient and modern, to create the powerful metaphors and tensions that compel this story on.

The.PowerBook (2000) tells the love story of a female narrator and her married female lover. It continues Winterson's experimentation with literary form, and, like *Oranges*, is concerned with 'love and gender, the knightly quest for the Grail and the journey that maps it' (Libby Brooks, 'Power Surge', the *Guardian Weekend*, 2 September 2000). Like her other fiction, *The.PowerBook* critiques the restrictiveness of marriage and examines issues of identity, storytelling and power. As critic Elaine Showalter writes: 'Designed to suggest the appearance and the technique of virtual reality, with a cover like a computer handbook and chapter divisions of hard drives, icons and documents, *The.PowerBook* is not a playful postmodern experiment or an investigation of the multiple personalities of e-mail. Instead, Winterson uses the metaphor of e-mail to discuss sexual freedom and power' ('Eternal Triangles', the *Guardian Review*, 2 September 2000).

Winterson has edited a collection of short stories called *Passion Fruit: Romantic Fiction with a Twist* (1986), published a collection of her own stories, *The World and Other Places* (1998), and has written a health and fitness book called *Fit for the Future: The Guide for Women Who Want to Live Well* (1986). Winterson has also written successfully for the screen. Her screenplay based on *Oranges* was televised in 1990 to great critical acclaim, winning a BAFTA award for best drama and a Royal Television Society award. Her film script *Great Moments in Aviation* was published in 1994. Through fairy-tale conventions, it offers new perspectives on familiar real-life stories of the emigration to England from the Caribbean. The focus is the boat journey of a black West Indian woman, Gabriel Angel, travelling to England in the late 1950s. It is preoccupied with the power of the imagination, with the idea of a quest to realise a dream, and with identity.

In all of Winterson's fiction attention is drawn to the way that identity is formed within a specific cultural context; social conventions and systems of belief, dominated by the institutions of marriage, the heterosexual family and the church, restrict freedom of expression. In particular, gender and sexuality are means of relating to the social and political structures in which an individual exists. By contrast, imagination, art and a passionate engagement with language can envision a more diverse, honest, liberated and liberating world, with fantasy opening up alternative ways of seeing and experiencing reality and offering alternative models for identity. The critical impulse in Winterson's work is broadly **feminist** and is pursued with exuberance and, frequently, scathing wit. The views of outsiders are often made central, and first person narratives of self-reflection are favoured over plot development.

Winterson has also written a collection of critical essays, *Art Objects: Essays on Ecstasy and Effrontery* (1995), in which she discusses her own writing and aesthetics, as well as the modernist writers who have influenced her work (notably Virginia Woolf, Gertrude Stein and T.S. Eliot). The title of the collection is ambiguous (is art an object, or does it object?) and the essays debate the function of art, in particular the notion that art should reflect or reproduce reality. As in her fiction, Winterson counters this idea of **mimeticism** and makes the case that art exposes the narrative structures through which we perceive and make sense of life, and simultaneously makes alternatives available.

HISTORICAL CONTEXT

The novel has two historical dimensions – the period in which it is set and the time at which it was written. The realist detail of the novel, with its references to post-war popular culture, to housing improvements (fitting bathrooms) and CB radios are suggestive of an era between the late 1950s and the 1970s. There is no hint of the 'swinging '60s', but a poor, working-class family in northern England, especially one engrossed in evangelical Christianity, would be far removed from the somewhat mythologised events of that decade.

The novel is also informed by the time at which it was written. Following the defeat of the miners' strike, the mid-1980s saw a consolidation of right-wing politics and an intensification of Prime Minister Margaret Thatcher's policies. Among other things, such policies effectively worked to turn the clock back in terms of women's social position. Individualism was fostered, nationalised industries were privatised, and a revival of traditional moral values was pursued. *Oranges* concerns itself with challenging injustices, exposing abuses of power, and undermining extreme right-wing views and rigidly enforced, narrow-minded moral values. Margaret Thatcher, along with her ministers Cecil Parkinson and Nicholas Ridley, are part of what Winterson calls her 'unholy trinity'.

However, Thatcherist politics prompted a reaction in the form of a broad front of left-wing activism (CND, green campaigns, TUC, Gay Liberation, and Rock Against Racism), which lent its support to the Women's Movement. Feminist publishing houses, growing since the 1960s, provided a forum for debate, created an increasingly important space for the publication of women's writing and generated an audience for it. In this context, writing by women began to flourish, and it is useful to see Winterson alongside other contemporary women writers, who were similarly experimenting with form and language to raise issues of gender politics and to expose and challenge the cultural conventions and social and political power structures that impact negatively on women in a material and psychological way. Writers such as Angela Carter, Michèle Roberts, Sara Maitland and Emma Tennant draw on and revise fairy tales and other cultural myths in order to raise questions about the formation of identity. They subversively blur the boundaries of realism and fantasy in an exploration of female subjectivity and sexuality. The double-edged power of language both to oppress and act as a tool in the imagining of alternative realities is a central concern, and the perspectives of marginalised figures, often women, are foregrounded.

Oranges can also be seen in the context of contemporary representations of girls and young women in fiction by writers such as Toni Morrison, Jamaica Kincaid and Carol Shields, where their success is not dependent on cultural conformity, but on resistance to social norms. Although Winterson insists that she is a writer who happens to be a lesbian rather than a lesbian who writes, it is useful to see *Oranges* in the context of other lesbian fiction of the 1970s and 1980s. In particular, Rita Mae Brown's coming-out novel, *Rubyfruit Jungle* (1974), provides some useful parallels. The heroine, Molly Bolt, is adopted into a provincial, extremely right-wing family and, like Jeanette, sees intolerance and not her lesbian sexuality as a problem. Like *Oranges,* the novel is humorous and Molly is a challenging and assertive heroine.

Winterson's writing has also been compared to the magic realism of Latin American writers Jorge Luis Borges and Gabriel Garcia Marquez, as well as to the post-modernist experiments of the Italian writer Italo Calvino. Critic Paulina Palmer, for instance, suggests that *The Passion* draws on Calvino's representation of Venice in *Invisible Cities*, shifting his masculinist perspective to a more feminist and lesbian one (in *Postmodern Studies 25*, eds Grice and Woods, 1998, pp. 113–4). Winterson's writing is also influenced by the poets of the English Renaissance, the visionary Romantic poets (Keats, Blake and Byron) and by other poets, such as Robert Graves. Winterson herself insists that knowledge of the literary past is a prerequisite for innovation and progress. She locates herself within a tradition of experimental writing developed by modernist writers in the first few decades of the twentieth century. In *Art Objects* she claims Virginia Woolf, Gertrude Stein and T.S. Eliot as influences inspiring her passion for innovation in language and form.

Part six

C RITICAL HISTORY & BROADER PERSPECTIVES

RECEPTION AND EARLY REVIEWS

Critic Lynne Pearce claims that 'Jeanette Winterson has come to represent the popular face of lesbian fiction' (*Volcanoes and Pearl Divers*, ed. Suzanne Raitt, 1995, p. 147). However, *Oranges Are Not the Only Fruit* is a novel that has a broad appeal; it has enjoyed success with a number of different audiences, winning great acclaim and the Whitbread Prize for a first novel in 1985. Its originality, literary quality and humour were repeatedly praised by reviewers – mainstream, lesbian and feminist. When Winterson later adapted her novel for television, the drama met with a similarly positive response, winning a BAFTA award for best drama and a silver medal at Cannes for best script. Again, viewers and critics of all persuasions responded positively.

Explanations for this success centre on the fact that the novel seems to invite and can sustain diverse readings, from the liberal humanist reading of Jeanette's experience as universal (a 'typical' story about the familial tensions and conflicts with authority figures experienced by most people as they grow up) to the specifically lesbian reading (as a 'coming-out' story). In her introduction to the novel, Winterson herself seems to address this diverse appeal in her claims that *Oranges* is 'experimental... threatening' and, apparently paradoxically, 'comforting' in its 'dealing with the emotions and confrontations that none of us can avoid' (pp. xiii, xiv). Many critics have explored this diverse appeal. For instance, Lynne Pearce looks at the way that the story of romantic love in *Oranges* can be read as a universal experience, transcending the specifics of history, gender and cultural context, or as a political engagement with the powerful **ideology** of romantic love. Hilary Hinds also considers the different ways both novel and drama have been read, and explores the phenomenal popular appeal of this unapologetic lesbian text.

In general, the reception of Winterson's fiction has been equivocal. Many critics and reviewers find the writing exciting, innovative, interesting and intellectually and emotionally stimulating; others find it derivative, contradictory and occasionally offensive. However, *Oranges* and Winterson's later fiction have stimulated a body of critical material that is continuing to grow. Some of the key and recurrent critical ways of reading *Oranges* explore the novel's ambivalent status as **autobiographical fiction**, analyse its **intertextual** and parodic elements, and examine the interplay of **realism** and **magic realism**, fantasy and fairy tale. The majority of critical readings take a broadly feminist approach, exploring the ways the novel can be seen to offer a critique of social conventions and cultural norms; much of the criticism also employs **post-structuralist** critical theory, and sees the novel as engaging with **post-modernist** aesthetics and philosophical concerns.

FEMINIST APPROACHES

Feminist critical approaches to the novel are diverse, embracing a spectrum of theoretical positions, including Marxist, post-structuralist and psychoanalytic. Such feminist readings range from those focused on the effect of the material, social, political and economic conditions depicted in the novel, to those that focus on the linguistic, **metaphysical** and psychoanalytical structures.

Drawing comparisons with Rita Mae Brown's lesbian feminist coming-out novel, *Rubyfruit Jungle* (1973), Gabriele Griffin in *Heavenly Love* (1993) locates *Oranges* as part of an evolving tradition of lesbian literature. She considers only the realist elements of the novel, and views its representation of lesbianism as a reflection of the specific historical, political and cultural context in which the novel was produced. Griffin sees lesbian identity in the novel as natural, a given, although she also acknowledges that Jeanette's identity is moulded in relation to the community of which she is a part. She reads *Oranges Are Not the Only Fruit* as a lesbian *Bildungsroman*, and points to the social and political changes that have enabled a defiant lesbian heroine to emerge in literature. Typical of this and other feminist readings is the focus on the mother–daughter relationship.

Isabel C. Anievas Gamallo also considers *Oranges* as a lesbian *Bildungsroman*, but, unlike Griffin, takes a **post-structuralist** approach when examining the importance of cultural narratives in the construction of identity. She argues that although *Oranges* in many ways resembles the 'archetypal plot of the *Bildungsroman*' (with the hero embarking on a quest of self-discovery and returning home when his initiation into the adult world is successful and complete), the novel also subverts the traditionally male-centred narrative of social conformity (in *The Girl*, ed. Saxton, p. 122). Gamallo emphasises the centrality of the process of storytelling to the 'construction of lesbian girlhood' in *Oranges* (ibid., p. 119). The employment of a multiplicity of stories – fantastic, mythic and fairy tale – brings about a defiant disruption of the conventions of gender and sexuality, conventions that are reinforced in the traditional *Bildungsroman*. In this way the novel refuses to give a single, definitive interpretation of Jeanette's identity, and offers the reader only uncertainty, ambiguity and openness.

Like Griffin, Gamallo views the plot of the novel as a subversive version of the traditional *Bildungsroman*, as a lesbian 'coming-out' narrative, and also comments on the novel's location in a tradition of comic lesbian fiction. However, taking a post-structuralist approach, she emphasises the important role of stories in the understanding and representation of reality and experience. She suggests that the proliferation of stories and the parodic mimicry of 'authoritative and righteous patriarchal discourses, from romance, fable and myth, to the sacred language of the Bible' destabilises the idea of identity and subjectivity (ibid., p. 126). Her reading of Jeanette's subjectivity corresponds to the post-structuralist idea of the subject as an unstable network of discourses; in contrast to the liberal humanist idea of identity as a unified whole, 'the self becomes a constantly shifting entity, a product of languages and narratives, and ultimately a narrative in itself' (ibid., p. 127).

Lynne Pearce also offers a post-structuralist reading of the novel, focusing on the powerful and pervasive **ideological discourse** of romantic love and the way it affects our experience of events. Pearce argues that 'the experience of "being in love" depends entirely on the stories we find ourselves able to tell' (*Volcanoes and Pearl Divers*, ed. Raitt, pp. 154–5). Even as we think our response to experiences is unique, post-structuralist approaches to culture tell us it is 'already written' and that we simply follow a cultural script, a pattern we cannot entirely escape from. One way to avoid falling helpless victim to such ideological forces, Pearce suggests, is to treat romantic love with **irony**, to expose it as a fiction, and to reorganise its discursive elements in order to tell the love story differently.

The narrative model for romantic love in Western culture is unequivocally heterosexual, and Pearce argues that Winterson's re-writing of romantic love involves not an oppositional revision, 'pitting [heterosexual romantic love] against the specificities of lesbian "lived" experience', but the insertion of incongruous details of character and context in order to disrupt romantic narrative conventions. She cites the absurdity of the initiating scene of Jeanette and Melanie's romantic love story (eyes meeting across a crowded market fish stall) and of the lovers themselves (Jeanette in her newly purchased bright pink mac and Melanie diligently boning and gutting kippers) as a crucial disruption of the seriousness of romantic discourse. This immediately places this lesbian romance at odds with the conventional heterosexual romantic discourse, 'opens up a gap' between this lesbian love story and the more conventional narrative in a way that brings the political implications of two working-class girls falling in love to the fore.

Pearce argues that the **metafictional** emphasis on the fact that the realist love story being told in *Oranges* is just that, a story, a fiction, and the emphasis on the power of Winterson's characters to 'tell stories differently' suggest a resistance to being permanently bound to the prevalent single and all-encompassing heterosexual version of romantic experience. She reads the development of the romance between Jeanette and Melanie in the light of post-structuralist theorist Roland Barthes' text, *A Lover's Discourse*, and suggests the way that the discourse of romantic love in *Oranges* is given new meaning and significance.

FEMINIST PSYCHOANALYTIC APPROACHES

Traditional psychoanalytical (Freudian) narratives of psychosexual development posit a break from the mother as the crucial moment of entry into independent adulthood, a break that marks the end of what Freud calls the 'oedipal phase'. This process of maturation is echoed and concretised in simple narratives of development (fairy tales) and in more complex narratives of development (such as the *Bildungsroman*). However, it was recognised (tentatively by Freud and more explicitly by feminist psychoanalysts) that the male oedipal model is inadequate to describe the far more complex process of maturation that women undergo. For women, the break with the mother and the exit from the oedipal phase is not complete, and feminist psychoanalysts have argued that continued connection or a return to the mother is part of a woman's psychological process of maturation.

Starting from the premise that literary models of development that 'play out the dynamics of the oedipal phase' are inappropriate as paradigms for women's literary and psychosexual narratives of development, Laurel Bollinger argues that in *Oranges* Winterson uses **post-modern parody** of a range of biblical and non-biblical stories to create a model for Jeanette's narrative of lesbian maturity. This maintains the importance of Jeanette's quest for love and also her continued connection with her mother (*Tulsa Studies in Women's Literature*, 13 (2), p. 363). In particular, she examines Winterson's lesbian appropriation of the thematic elements of female loyalty, solidarity and devotion, as well as the basic plot element of return to the mother, from the Book of Ruth, as a paradigmatic text for the novel as a whole. Arguing that the biblical story of Ruth and Naomi has fairy-tale qualities anyway, Bollinger claims this as an appropriate literary model to express a woman's psychosexual and psychosocial development. She suggests that Winterson's appropriation of the bond between Ruth and Naomi, a central facet of which is the conversion of one woman to the other's faith, acts as a model for Jeanette's connection to her mother as well as to her lesbian lovers. It also acts as a model for her quest for faithfulness. She concludes that Winterson has created 'a feminist family romance', which revises Freudian models of psychosexual development by making the continuation of the mother–daughter bond central to the development of female subjectivity and process of maturation (ibid., p. 377).

World events	Author's life	Literary events
1950 Korean War begins		
1952 Test explosion of Britain's first atomic weapon		
1953 Coronation of Queen Elizabeth II; Sir Edmund Hillary and Sherpa Tenzing scale Mount Everest		**1953** Winston Churchill awarded Nobel Prize for Literature
1954 Food rationing officially ends in GB; Roger Bannister runs mile in under four minutes		
1956 First atomic power station opens in GB		
1957 Queen's Christmas broadcast televised for first time		
1958 First CND protest march from London to Aldermaston		
1959 First section of M1 motorway opened	**1959** Jeanette Winterson born in Manchester; adopted by Constance and Jack Winterson, Pentecostal evangelists	
1960 Sharpeville massacre in South Africa, 67 shot dead by police; John F. Kennedy elected president of the USA		**1960** Penguin Books prosecuted under Obscene Publications Act for publishing *Lady Chatterley's Lover* by D.H. Lawrence
1961 Yuri Gagarin becomes first man into space		**1961** Publication of *New English Bible* (New Testament)
1962 First live television transmission between USA and Europe		**1962** Doris Lessing, *The Golden Notebook*
1963 Death of Pope John XXIII; Great Train Robbery – £2.5 million stolen		

World events	Author's life	Literary events
1965 First US troops land in South Vietnam; first woman High Court judge appointed in Britain		
1966 England wins football World Cup		
1967 Outbreak of Six-day War in Middle East; first human heart transplant		**1967** Angela Carter, *The Magic Toyshop*
1969 Troops sent to quell conflict in Northern Ireland; voting age in UK lowered to 18; first men land on the moon		**1969** Margaret Atwood, *The Edible Woman*
		1970 Toni Morrison, *The Bluest Eye*
		1971 Germaine Greer, *The Female Eunuch*
		1972 Sir John Betjeman appointed Poet Laureate
1973 Three-day working week introduced to Britain to save fuel; Britain becomes member of EC; Vietnam War ends		**1973** Toni Morrison, *Sula*; Rita Mae Brown, *Rubyfruit Jungle*
1974 US Watergate scandal exposed		
	1975 Leaves parental home after beginning a relationship with another woman	**1975** Angela Carter, *The Bloody Chamber*
1978 World's first test-tube baby born in Britain	**1978-81** Attends St Catherine's College, Oxford, from which she graduates with a degree in English	
1979 Margaret Thatcher becomes Britain's first woman prime minister		**1979** Emma Tennant, *Wild Nights*
1980 Dissolution of Soviet empire begins		

World events	Author's life	Literary events
1981 Rioting breaks out in London, Liverpool and Manchester, apparently caused by conflict with the police		**1981** Salman Rushdie, *Midnight's Children*
1982 Falklands War begins	**1982** Employed at Roundhouse Theatre, London	**1982** Gabriel Garcia Marquez, Colombian writer of magic realist novels, wins Nobel Prize for Literature
1983 Women begin long-term anti-nuclear protest around US military base at Greenham Common, Berkshire; Cecil Parkinson resigns from Thatcher's Cabinet following disclosure of long-term affair with secretary	**1983** Editor at Brilliance Books	**1983** Michèle Roberts, *The Visitation*
1984 Year-long miners' strike begins against pit closures	**1984-5** Editor at Pandora Press	**1984** Angela Carter, *Nights at the Circus;* Michèle Roberts, *The Wild Girl*
1985 Live Aid concert in aid of famine relief in Africa	**1985** Publishes *Oranges Are Not the Only Fruit* (winner of the Whitbread Prize for best first fiction) and *Boating for Beginners*	**1985** Death of Italo Calvino; Margaret Atwood, *The Handmaid's Tale*
1986 Construction of Channel Tunnel begins	**1986** Publishes *The Passion* (winner of John Llewellyn Rhys Memorial Prize for the best writer under 35)	**1986** Death of Jorge Luis Borges, Argentinian writer, acclaimed exponent of magic realism
		1987 Toni Morrison, *Beloved*
1988 Women abseil into House of Commons in protest against Clause 28, which prohibits 'promotion' of homosexuality in schools		

World events	Author's life	Literary events
1989 Fall of the Berlin Wall; Boris Yeltsin wins landslide election in Russia, signalling the end of Communism	**1989** Publishes *Sexing the Cherry* (winner of E.M. Forster Award from American Academy of Arts and Letters)	**1989** Salman Rushdie goes into hiding, having been sentenced to death by Iranian religious leader for blasphemy in *The Satanic Verses*
1990 Margaret Thatcher resigns as prime minister; Nelson Mandela freed		
1991 Gulf War begins, following Iraq's invasion of Kuwait		
1992 Betty Boothroyd becomes first woman Speaker of the House of Commons; General Synod votes in favour of women priests	**1992** Publishes *Written on the Body*	
1994 Nelson Mandela becomes president of South Africa	**1994** Publishes *Art and Lies: A Piece for Three Voices and a Bard*; publishes *Great Moments in Aviation* (film script)	
	1995 Publishes *Art Objects: Essays in Ecstasy and Effrontery*	**1995** Pat Barker wins the Booker Prize for *The Ghost Road*
1996 Massacre of 16 schoolchildren in Dunblane, Scotland		
1997 Labour Party wins landslide victory in General Election; deaths of Diana, Princess of Wales and Mother Teresa	**1997** Publishes *Gut Symmetries*	
1998 Sex scandal erupts around President Clinton	**1998** Publishes *The World and Other Places* (short stories)	
	2000 Publishes *The.PowerBook*	

Laurel Bollinger, 'Models for Female Loyalty: The Biblical Ruth in Jeanette Winterson's *Oranges Are Not the Only Fruit*', in *Tulsa Studies in Women's Literature*, 13 (2), 1994

Ellen Brinks and Lee Talley, 'Unfamiliar Ties: Lesbian Constructions of Home and Family in Jeanette Winterson's *Oranges Are Not the Only Fruit* and Jewelle Gomez's *The Gilda Stories*', in *Homemaking: Women Writers and the Politics and Poetics of Home*, ed. Catherine Wiley and Fiona R. Barnes, Garland Publishing Inc., 1996

Tess Cosslett, 'Intertextuality in *Oranges Are Not the Only Fruit*: The Bible, Malory, and Jane Eyre', in *Postmodern Studies 25* (*'I'm telling you stories': Jeanette Winterson and the Politics of Reading*), eds Helena Grice and Tim Woods, Editions Rodopi, 1998

> Explores the ways that the intertextual stories in *Oranges* can be made to generate meanings in 'dialogue' with each other, maintaining an open, multiple, contradictory and ambiguous text which can serve feminist aims

Isabel C. Anievas Gamallo, 'Subversive Storytelling: The Construction of Lesbian Girlhood Through Fantasy and Fairy Tale in Jeanette Winterson's *Oranges Are Not the Only Fruit*', in *The Girl: Constructions of the Girl in Contemporary Fiction by Women*, ed. Ruth O. Saxton, Macmillan, 1998

Gabriele Griffin, *Heavenly Love?: Lesbian Images in Twentieth Century Women's Writing*, Manchester University Press, 1993

Hilary Hinds, '*Oranges Are Not the Only Fruit*: Reaching Audiences Other Lesbian Texts Cannot Reach', in *New Lesbian Criticism*, ed. Sally Munt, Harvester Wheatsheaf, 1992

Margaret Marshment and Julia Hallam, 'From String of Knots to Orange Box: Lesbians on Prime Time', in *The Good, the Bad and the Gorgeous: Popular Culture's Romance with Lesbianism*, eds Diane Hamer and Belinda Budge, Pandora, 1994

Paulina Palmer, in *Postmodern Studies 25*, 'The Passion: *Storytelling, Fantasy, Desire*', eds Helena Grice and Tim Woods, Editions Rodopi, 1998

Lynne Pearce, 'Written on Tablets of Stone? Jeanette Winterson, Roland Barthes, and the Discourse of Romantic Love', in *Volcanoes and*

Pearl Divers: Essays in Lesbian Feminist Studies, ed. Suzanne Raitt, Only Women Press, 1995

Lyn Pykett, 'A New Way with Words? Jeanette Winterson's Post-Modernism', in *Postmodern Studies 25* (*'I'm telling you stories': Jeanette Winterson and the Politics of Reading*), eds Helena Grice and Tim Woods, Editions Rodopi, 1998

> This collection of essays considers *Oranges* and other novels in the light of post-modern aesthetics and philosophical concerns

Susan Rubin Suleiman, 'Mothers and the Avant Garde: A Case of Mistaken Identity?', in *Avant Garde 4*, Editions Rodopi, 1990

Eleanor Wachtel, interview with Jeanette Winterson, *Malahat Review*, Spring 1997

allegory a narrative that has two levels of meaning, an explicit, literal level of meaning and a second hidden but coherent meaning. All interpretation of literature, any way of understanding a work as containing meanings other than those explicit on the level of its literal surface, can be called allegorical. Allegory can be distinguished from symbolism, although the two terms are often used in such a way that their meanings overlap. Symbols usually have a wider and more suggestive range of meaning, and a more obvious, less tenuous relationship with what they represent. Fables and parables are examples of allegorical narratives

allusion a passing reference in a work of literature to something outside itself. A writer may allude to legends, historical facts or personages, to other works of literature, or even to autobiographical details. Literary allusion describes the inclusion of passages or phrases from other literary texts, or the imitation or parody of another writer's style in order to introduce implicit contrasts or comparisons

association first used in its special philosophical sense by John Locke (1632–1704), 'association' refers to the mental connection between an object and ideas that have some relation to it. Philosopher David Hume (1711–76) extended the meaning of the word to include the sometimes arbitrary relationships between ideas in the mind. Twentieth-century psychoanalysts use free association of ideas as a means of exploring the subconscious mind

autobiographical fiction narratives written in the first person, which rely heavily on autobiographical style, or which parody that style

Bildungsroman a novel that describes the protagonist's development from childhood to maturity. This development usually involves a spiritual crisis, and tends to focus on the relationship between experience, education, character and identity

binary opposition the fundamental contrasts (such as in/out, off/on, good/bad) used in structuralist methods of linguistic analysis, and in criticism, anthropology and feminism. It has been argued that binarism is fundamental to all learning and interpretation of experience, and that all processes of understanding involve discrimination and choice between opposed possibilities. Feminists point out that the lists of binary oppositions (such as active/passive, head/heart, reason/feeling, strength/weakness) often coincide with the male/female opposition, with the masculine side of the opposition having more intrinsic value in male-dominated societies

deconstruction a blanket term for certain radical critical theories which revise and develop structuralism. Many of its ideas originate in the post-structuralist linguistic philosophy developed by Jacques Derrida, and it has had a strong influence on literary and critical theory. It is premised on the idea that meaning is not inherent in words, but depends on relationships between words within the system of language. It claims that all writing is intertextual and 'already written', and therefore not free from the effects of factors such as race, gender, class and literary institutions in its generation of meaning. Deconstruction playfully challenges traditional approaches to criticism: it offers an alternative method of analysing texts, which assumes that neither language nor literary text have stable or fixed meanings. In deconstructive readings, meanings are multiple, and contradiction, ambiguity and word-play are key elements of interpretation

dialogic text a text that allows the expression of various points of view in the manner of a dialogue in drama, leaving the reader with open questions

discourse traditionally, conversation, or a serious discussion or examination of a learned topic. In general, discourse refers to the 'how' of a narrative as opposed to its 'what'. The term can be used to refer to any self-contained body of ideas, opinions, approaches and methods, and the language that contains them. It is a framework of references commonly used in relation to a particular topic; different discourses will have quite separate ways of using language, with different expectations of what their audiences will know and expect, different kinds of grammar and argument, different jargons. Considering examples of the 'discursive practices' of a group ties language to its social context rather than considering it in abstraction. Literature contains many different discourses of this kind, and in its entirety is itself a discourse, using particular kinds of language in particular ways

feminism broadly speaking, a political movement claiming political power and economic equality of women with men. Feminist criticism and scholarship seek to explore and expose the masculine bias in texts and to challenge stereotypical representations of women in literature, as well as to 'recover' the many women writers and texts ignored by the male-biased canon. Since the late 1960s, feminist theories about literature and language, and feminist interpretations of texts, have multiplied enormously and now there is an extensive range of feminist approaches which engage productively with many other theoretical approaches

foreshadow to suggest in advance what will happen later

ideology the collection of ideas, opinions, values, beliefs and preconceptions that go to make up the mind-set of a group of people, that is, the intellectual framework through which they view everything, and which colours all their attitudes and feelings (especially, perhaps, assumptions about power and authority). What we take to be reality is controlled by the ideologies of the era in which we live

imagery a critical word with several different applications. In its narrowest sense, an image is a word-picture, a description of some visible scene or object. More commonly, however, imagery refers to the figurative language in a piece of literature (metaphors and similes), or all the words that refer to objects and qualities that appeal to the senses and feelings. Thematic imagery recurs throughout a work of art and is used to underpin the themes; in *Oranges*, for example, wall and thread imagery underpin the themes of exile and return

intertext structuralism argues that a text is a system in which language does not refer to reality but only to itself and the patterns created within (inter) the text. Literature as a whole is also perceived as a self-referential system or structure. Intertextuality is a term used to refer to the many and various kinds of relationship that exist between texts, such as adaptation, translation, imitation, allusion, plagiarism and parody

irony consists of saying one thing and meaning another; it is ironic when the implicit meaning of what is said differs from the surface or apparent meaning. Irony is generated when there is an incongruity between what is expected or assumed and what is actually the case, or what seems to be the case. Dramatic irony is a device that allows the reader to possess more information about what is happening than some of the characters themselves have. Characters may also speak in a dramatically ironic way, saying something that points to events to come without realising the significance of their words

juxtapose to place close together for contrast

magic realism fiction that mixes and disrupts ordinary, everyday realism with strange, 'impossible' and miraculous episodes and powers; Angela Carter created a particular kind of magic realism, which reworks folk and fairy tales and mixes the modern and the mythical

melodrama the most common critical use of the words 'melodrama' or 'melodramatic' is to characterise any kind of writing that relies on sensational happenings, violent action and improbable events

metafiction fiction about fiction; it draws attention to itself as fiction, to the act of fiction-making and to the process of reading in order to raise questions about the relationship between reality and fiction; metafiction challenges realist conventions, which work to conceal the gap between art and life, by highlighting the artificiality of all literary conventions

metaphor an implied comparison, e.g. She sailed into the room; this does not directly compare two things, but suggests a likeness (here, between a woman and a ship) without using the words 'like' or 'as' (see also simile)

metaphysics branch of philosophy that deals with the nature of existence, reality and experience

mimesis term used by Aristotle in his *Poetics* (fourth century BC), when he states that tragedy is an 'imitation' of an action. Mimetic criticism regards literature as imitating or reflecting life, and therefore emphasises the truth and accuracy of its representation, its realism in a general sense

pastiche a work of art made up of fragments of an original

patriarchy a social and political system organised so as to give power and prestige to men, and likely to be regarded by men as the natural order of things. A term frequently used in feminist criticism

physics the science of energy, matter, motion and force

plot the plan of a literary work, especially in drama or fiction. To reveal the plot of a novel involves something more than simply explaining the sequence of events: 'plot' suggests a pattern of relationships between events, a web of causation; this happens because of that, and so on

pluralism a term much used in post-structuralist criticism to indicate the openness of texts to many different interpretations; all texts are open to the play of innumerable meanings, rendering the search for meaning infinitely extendable

post-modernism a slippery term, which refers to aesthetic qualities and philosophical concerns. Magpie borrowings of former styles are characteristic of post-modern style. Such borrowings can be witty and clever, making a statement about pluralism, tolerance and eclecticism, as well as revealing limitations inherent in former literary conventions and methods. Other characteristics of post-modern fiction include pastiche of earlier styles and forms, a mingling of historically real and fictional characters, a mixing of realist and fantasy modes (as in magic realism), and metafictional techniques and elements. Post-modern texts are often organised to reveal the instability of language, and to show the reader how particular meanings and values are temporary and self-generated constructions

post-modern parody parodists take texts considered to be 'proper' literature and repeat material from them, treating it with irony in order to confront the literary tradition and to explore their relationship to it; an approach most valuable to those outside the tradition and marginalised in society. Jeanette, marginalised from the heterosexual mainstream of secular society and the church, parodies 'official' texts in order to confront and explore her relationship to them

post-structuralism builds on and refines structuralism Deconstruction is a significant post-structuralist development

psychoanalytic criticism drawing on Sigmund Freud's theories of psychoanalysis (which themselves referred heavily to literature and the creative process for illustration and demonstration), psychoanalytic criticism analyses literature according to theories of the mind. More recently, Jacques Lacan has reworked Freud's psychological theories in terms of structuralism, arguing that the mind is organised around a system of differences, like a language

realism a term used in two main ways: to describe the trend in nineteenth-century literature, especially in prose fiction, which aimed at presenting new truths about people in society in a non-ideal or non-romantic way; to describe a way of representing real life in literature, which is associated with this historical period

register apart from its meaning as a list of names, 'register' is used by literary critics to denote the kind of language being used, especially as appropriate to a particular situation. For example, an author of children's books will use language of a different register from a writer of technical manuals

rhetoric language designed to persuade or impress, now often used pejoratively to imply empty or false attempts at persuasion

roman-à-clef a novel in which some of the characters are thinly disguised portraits of real, famous people

simile a figure of speech in which one thing is said to be like another; similes always contain the words 'like' or 'as'. Whereas metaphor merely suggests a comparison, simile keeps the comparison explicit. For example, 'black peas look like rabbit droppings' (p. 6)

structuralism dismisses the idea that language is natural and can be used unproblematically as a mirror to reality. Structuralists see language not as a neutral means of communication, but as a self-enclosed system and as a code. A basic tenet of structuralism is that meaning is not inherent in words, but depends on their mutual relationships within the system of language, a system based on difference. Structuralism argues that a text is a system in which language does not refer to reality but only to itself and the patterns created within the text. Literature as a whole is also perceived as a self-referential system or structure and literary texts refer to each other (see intertext)

symbol something that represents something else (often an idea or a quality) by analogy or association. Thus white, lion and rose commonly symbolise or represent innocence, courage and beauty respectively. Such symbols exist by convention and tradition. Writers use conventional symbols, but they also invent their own. The particular objects, scenes or episodes that come to stand for the major themes of the work may be repeated or mirrored in many different ways so as to give the work a symbolic structure, e.g. oranges as a substitute for mother love

theme the abstract subject of a work; its central idea or ideas, which may or may not be explicit or obvious. A text may contain several themes or thematic interests

verisimilitude the appearance of truth or reality; in literature it arises from the author's skill in depicting things realistically. Verisimilitude depends not on any direct relationship with reality, but more on a collection of literary conventions, arising from the choice of certain kinds of material and approach, and the avoidance of obvious improbabilities

vernacular the language of one's homeland; also used to describe dialects (local speech), or even rough, earthy speech

Author of this note

Kathryn Simpson is a Lecturer in English at Birmingham University, Westhill. She has taught at Wolverhamptom University and Birmingham University School of Continuing Studies, as well as in a number of colleges of further education. She received her BA and PhD in English from Birmingham University.

York Notes Advanced (£3.99 each)

Margaret Atwood
Cat's Eye

Margaret Atwood
The Handmaid's Tale

Jane Austen
Mansfield Park

Jane Austen
Persuasion

Jane Austen
Pride and Prejudice

Alan Bennett
Talking Heads

William Blake
Songs of Innocence and of Experience

Charlotte Brontë
Jane Eyre

Emily Brontë
Wuthering Heights

Angela Carter
Nights at the Circus

Geoffrey Chaucer
The Franklin's Prologue and Tale

Geoffrey Chaucer
The Miller's Prologue and Tale

Geoffrey Chaucer
Prologue To the Canterbury Tales

Geoffrey Chaucer
The Wife of Bath's Prologue and Tale

Samuel Taylor Coleridge
Selected Poems

Joseph Conrad
Heart of Darkness

Daniel Defoe
Moll Flanders

Charles Dickens
Great Expectations

Charles Dickens
Hard Times

Emily Dickinson
Selected Poems

John Donne
Selected Poems

Carol Ann Duffy
Selected Poems

George Eliot
Middlemarch

George Eliot
The Mill on the Floss

T.S. Eliot
Selected Poems

F. Scott Fitzgerald
The Great Gatsby

E.M. Forster
A Passage to India

Brian Friel
Translations

Thomas Hardy
The Mayor of Casterbridge

Thomas Hardy
The Return of the Native

Thomas Hardy
Selected Poems

Thomas Hardy
Tess of the d'Urbervilles

Seamus Heaney
Selected Poems from Opened Ground

Nathaniel Hawthorne
The Scarlet Letter

Kazuo Ishiguro
The Remains of the Day

Ben Jonson
The Alchemist

James Joyce
Dubliners

John Keats
Selected Poems

Christopher Marlowe
Doctor Faustus

Arthur Miller
Death of a Salesman

John Milton
Paradise Lost Books I & II

Toni Morrison
Beloved

Sylvia Plath
Selected Poems

Alexander Pope
Rape of the Lock and other poems

William Shakespeare
Antony and Cleopatra

William Shakespeare
As You Like It

William Shakespeare
Hamlet

William Shakespeare
King Lear

William Shakespeare
Measure for Measure

William Shakespeare
The Merchant of Venice

William Shakespeare
A Midsummer Night's Dream

William Shakespeare
Much Ado About Nothing

William Shakespeare
Othello

William Shakespeare
Richard II

William Shakespeare
Romeo and Juliet

William Shakespeare
The Taming of the Shrew

William Shakespeare
The Tempest

William Shakespeare
Twelfth Night

William Shakespeare
The Winter's Tale

George Bernard Shaw
Saint Joan

Mary Shelley
Frankenstein

Jonathan Swift
Gulliver's Travels and A Modest Proposal

Alfred, Lord Tennyson
Selected Poems

Alice Walker
The Color Purple

Oscar Wilde
The Importance of Being Earnest

Tennessee Williams
A Streetcar Named Desire

John Webster
The Duchess of Malfi

Virginia Woolf
To the Lighthouse

W.B. Yeats
Selected Poems

GCSE and equivalent levels (£3.50 each)

Maya Angelou
I Know Why the Caged Bird Sings

Jane Austen
Pride and Prejudice

Alan Ayckbourn
Absent Friends

Elizabeth Barrett Browning
Selected Poems

Robert Bolt
A Man for All Seasons

Harold Brighouse
Hobson's Choice

Charlotte Brontë
Jane Eyre

Emily Brontë
Wuthering Heights

Shelagh Delaney
A Taste of Honey

Charles Dickens
David Copperfield

Charles Dickens
Great Expectations

Charles Dickens
Hard Times

Charles Dickens
Oliver Twist

Roddy Doyle
Paddy Clarke Ha Ha Ha

George Eliot
Silas Marner

George Eliot
The Mill on the Floss

Anne Frank
The Diary of Anne Frank

William Golding
Lord of the Flies

Oliver Goldsmith
She Stoops To Conquer

Willis Hall
The Long and the Short and the Tall

Thomas Hardy
Far from the Madding Crowd

Thomas Hardy
The Mayor of Casterbridge

Thomas Hardy
Tess of the d'Urbervilles

Thomas Hardy
The Withered Arm and other Wessex Tales

L.P. Hartley
The Go-Between

Seamus Heaney
Selected Poems

Susan Hill
I'm the King of the Castle

Barry Hines
A Kestrel for a Knave

Louise Lawrence
Children of the Dust

Harper Lee
To Kill a Mockingbird

Laurie Lee
Cider with Rosie

Arthur Miller
The Crucible

Arthur Miller
A View from the Bridge

Robert O'Brien
Z for Zachariah

Frank O'Connor
My Oedipus Complex and Other Stories

George Orwell
Animal Farm

J.B. Priestley
An Inspector Calls

J.B. Priestley
When We Are Married

Willy Russell
Educating Rita

Willy Russell
Our Day Out

J.D. Salinger
The Catcher in the Rye

William Shakespeare
Henry IV Part 1

William Shakespeare
Henry V

William Shakespeare
Julius Caesar

William Shakespeare
Macbeth

William Shakespeare
The Merchant of Venice

William Shakespeare
A Midsummer Night's Dream

William Shakespeare
Much Ado About Nothing

William Shakespeare
Romeo and Juliet

William Shakespeare
The Tempest

William Shakespeare
Twelfth Night

George Bernard Shaw
Pygmalion

Mary Shelley
Frankenstein

R.C. Sherriff
Journey's End

Rukshana Smith
Salt on the Snow

John Steinbeck
Of Mice and Men

Robert Louis Stevenson
Dr Jekyll and Mr Hyde

Jonathan Swift
Gulliver's Travels

Robert Swindells
Daz 4 Zoe

Mildred D. Taylor
Roll of Thunder, Hear My Cry

Mark Twain
Huckleberry Finn

James Watson
Talking in Whispers

Edith Wharton
Ethan Frome

William Wordsworth
Selected Poems

A Choice of Poets

Mystery Stories of the Nineteenth Century including The Signalman

Nineteenth Century Short Stories

Poetry of the First World War

Six Women Poets